SPY STORY GRAPHICS

AGENTS OF INDEPENDENCE

DARING SPIES OF THE AMERICAN REVOLUTION

BY MATTHEW K. MANNING

ILLUSTRATED BY DANTE GINEVRA

CAPSTONE PRESS
a capstone imprint

Published by Capstone Press, an imprint of Capstone.
1710 Roe Crest Drive
North Mankato, Minnesota 56003
capstonepub.com

Library of Congress Cataloging-in-Publication data is
available on the Library of Congress website.

ISBN: 9781669085584 (hardcover)
ISBN: 9781669085836 (paperback)
ISBN: 9781669085577 (ebook PDF)

Summary: America's first president masterminds a
network of spies. A young officer creates a clever spy
ring. A patriotic woman uses her laundry as a secret code.
These thrilling, true stories of espionage shifted the course
of the American Revolution. How did these daring spies
manage to outfox the British and contribute to the fight for
independence?

Editorial Credits:
Editor: Donald Lemke; Designer: Kay Fraser;
Production Specialist: Katy LaVigne

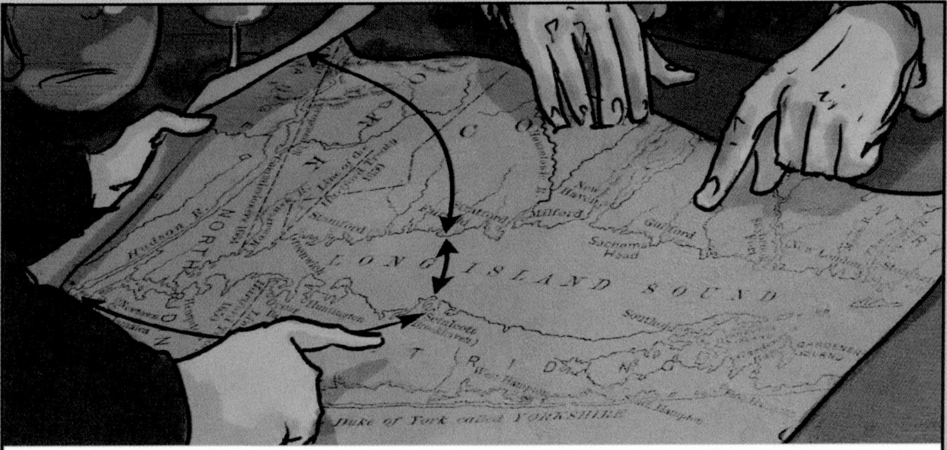

LONG ISLAND SOUND

TABLE OF CONTENTS

INTRODUCTION
THE REVOLUTION

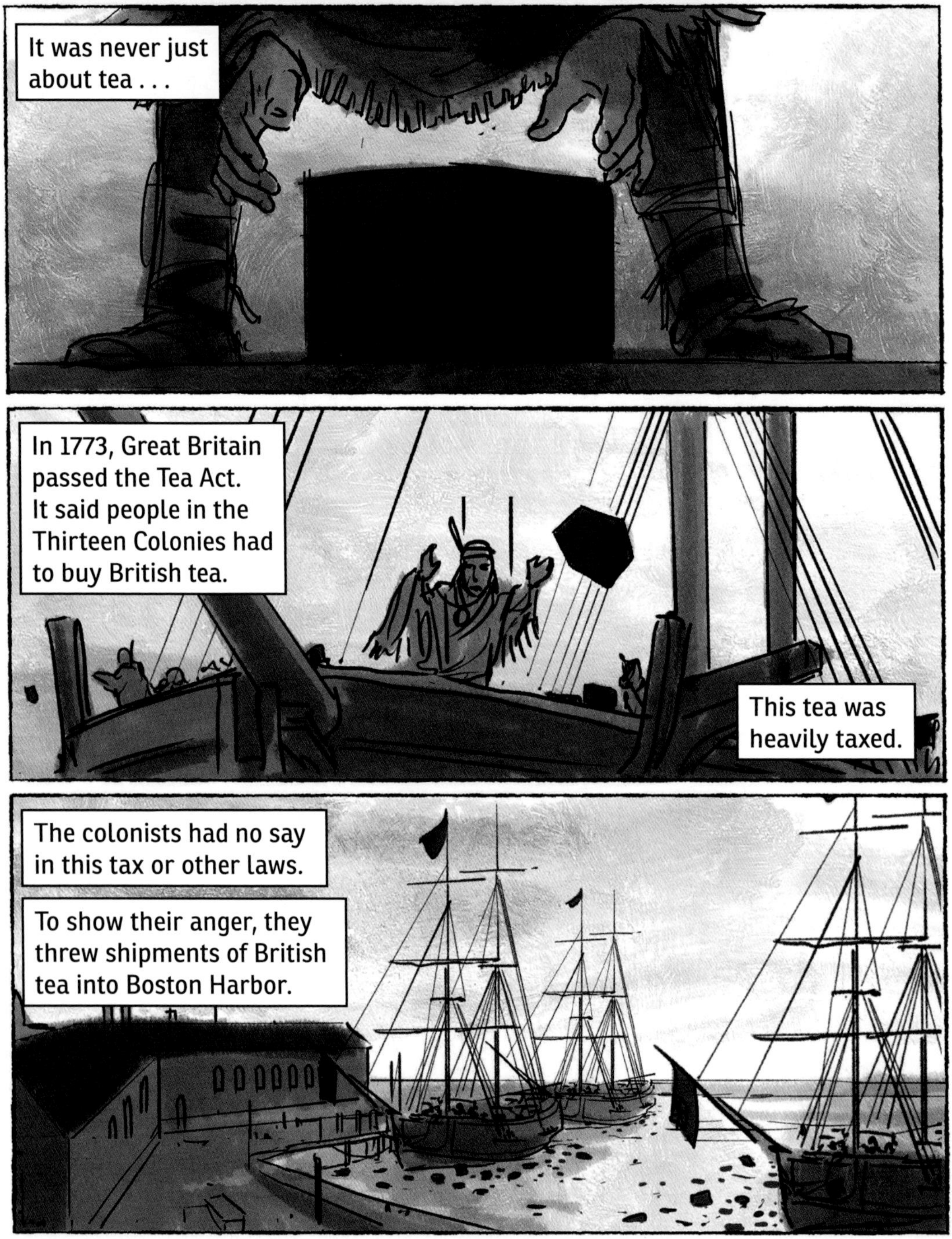

It was never just about tea . . .
In 1773, Great Britain passed the Tea Act. It said people in the Thirteen Colonies had to buy British tea.
This tea was heavily taxed.
The colonists had no say in this tax or other laws.
To show their anger, they threw shipments of British tea into Boston Harbor.

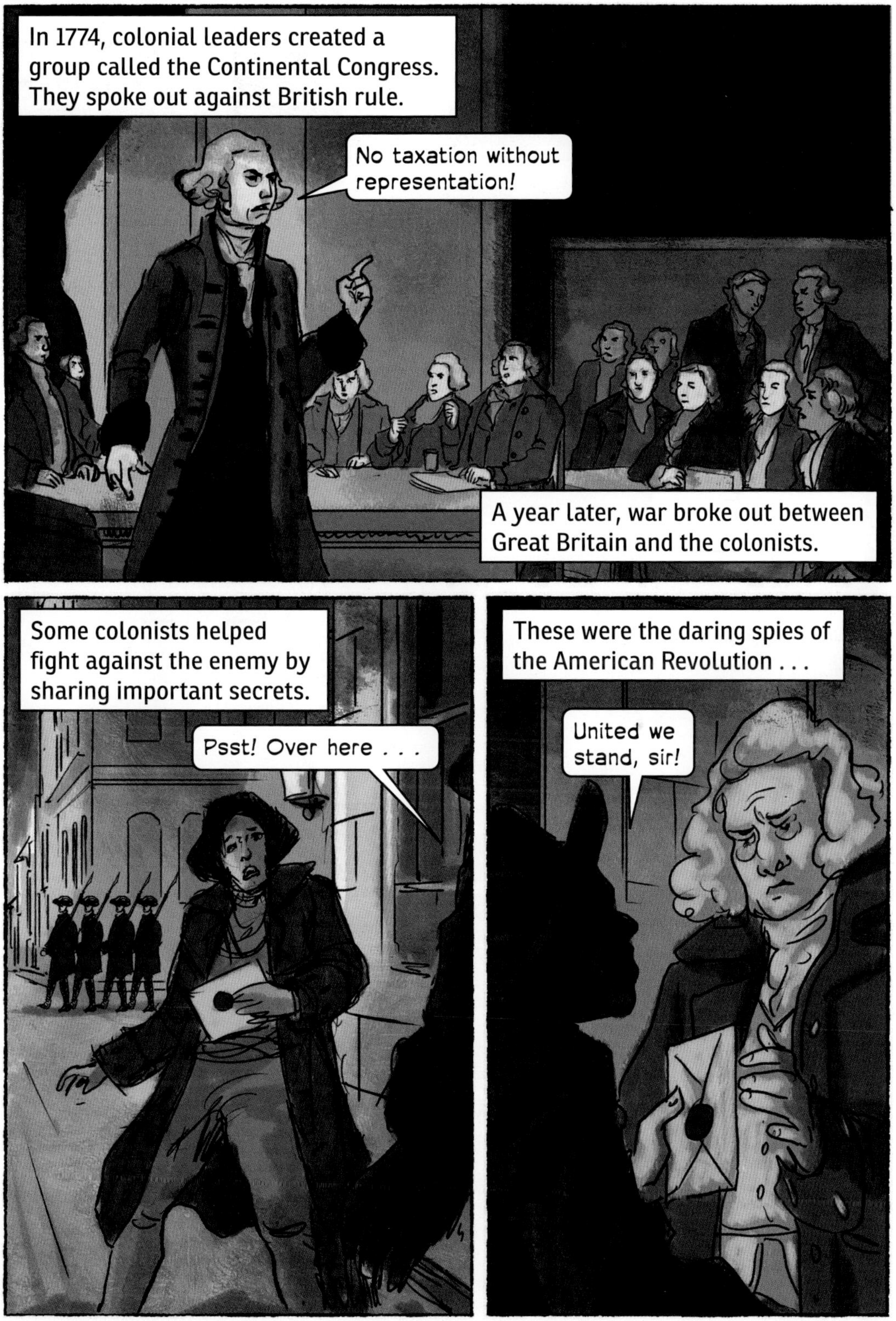
In 1774, colonial leaders created a group called the Continental Congress. They spoke out against British rule.
No taxation without representation!
A year later, war broke out between Great Britain and the colonists.
Some colonists helped fight against the enemy by sharing important secrets.
Psst! Over here . . .
These were the daring spies of the American Revolution . . .
United we stand, sir!

CHAPTER ONE

GEORGE WASHINGTON: THE FIRST SPYMASTER

He is known today as the man on the United States quarter . . .

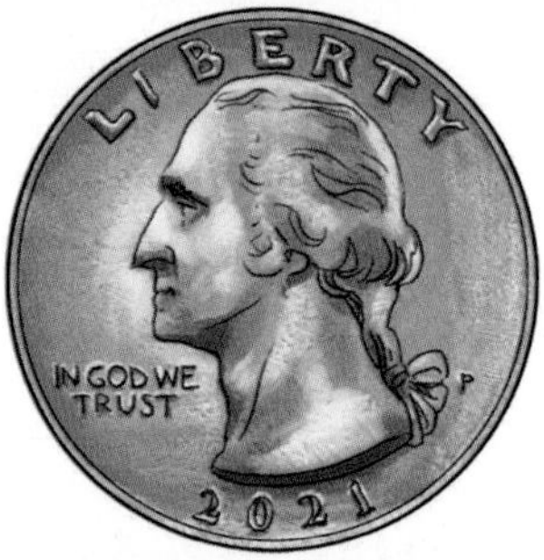
LIBERTY
IN GOD WE TRUST
P
2021

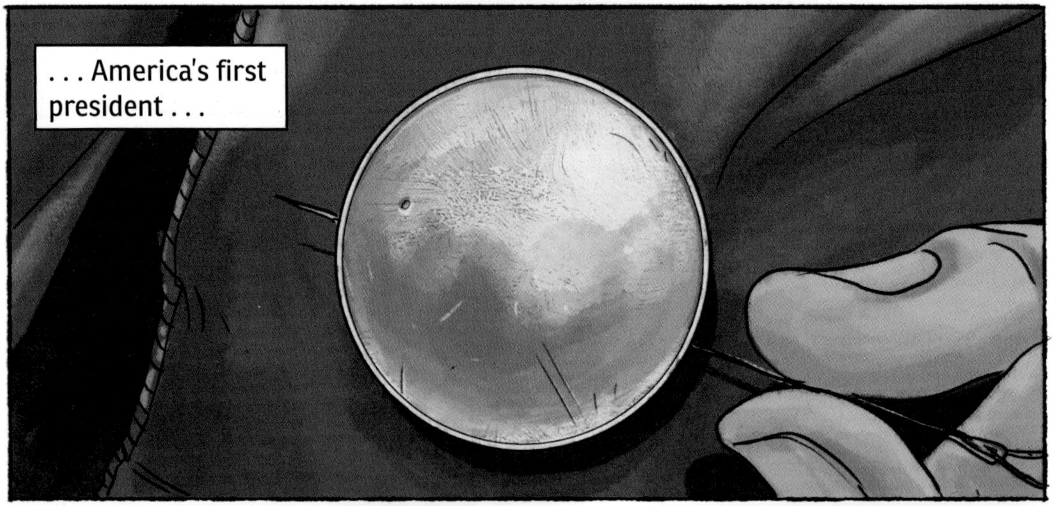
. . . America's first president . . .

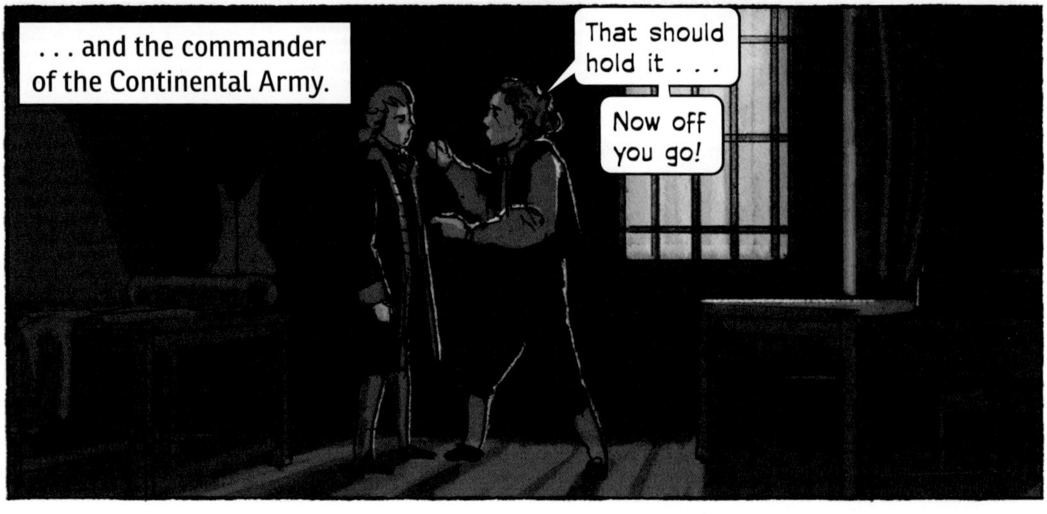
. . . and the commander of the Continental Army.
That should hold it . . .
Now off you go!

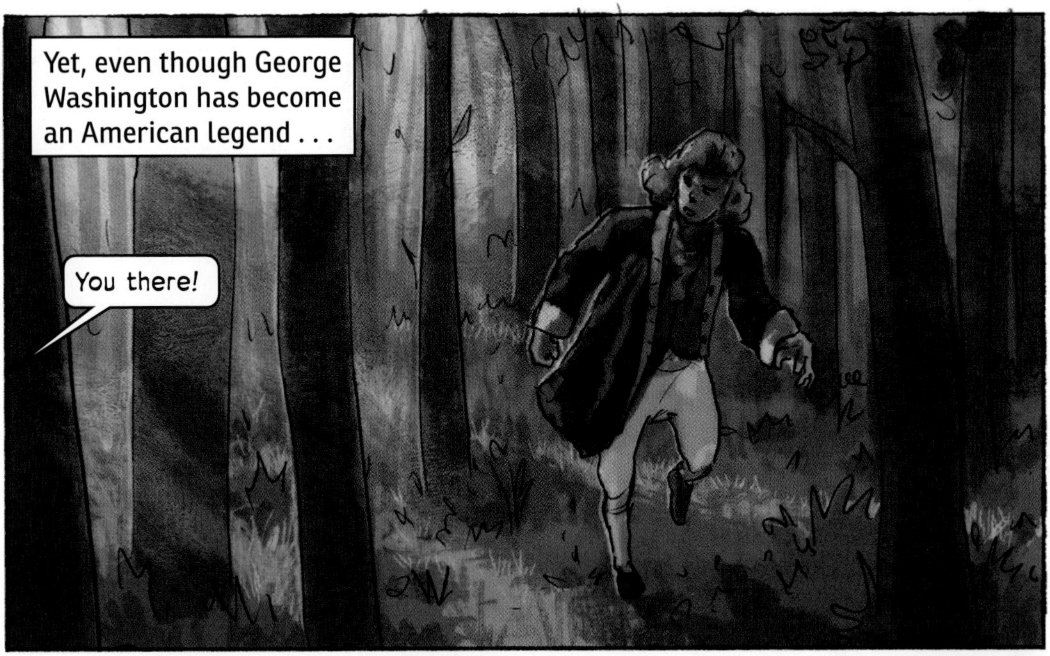
Yet, even though George Washington has become an American legend . . .
You there!

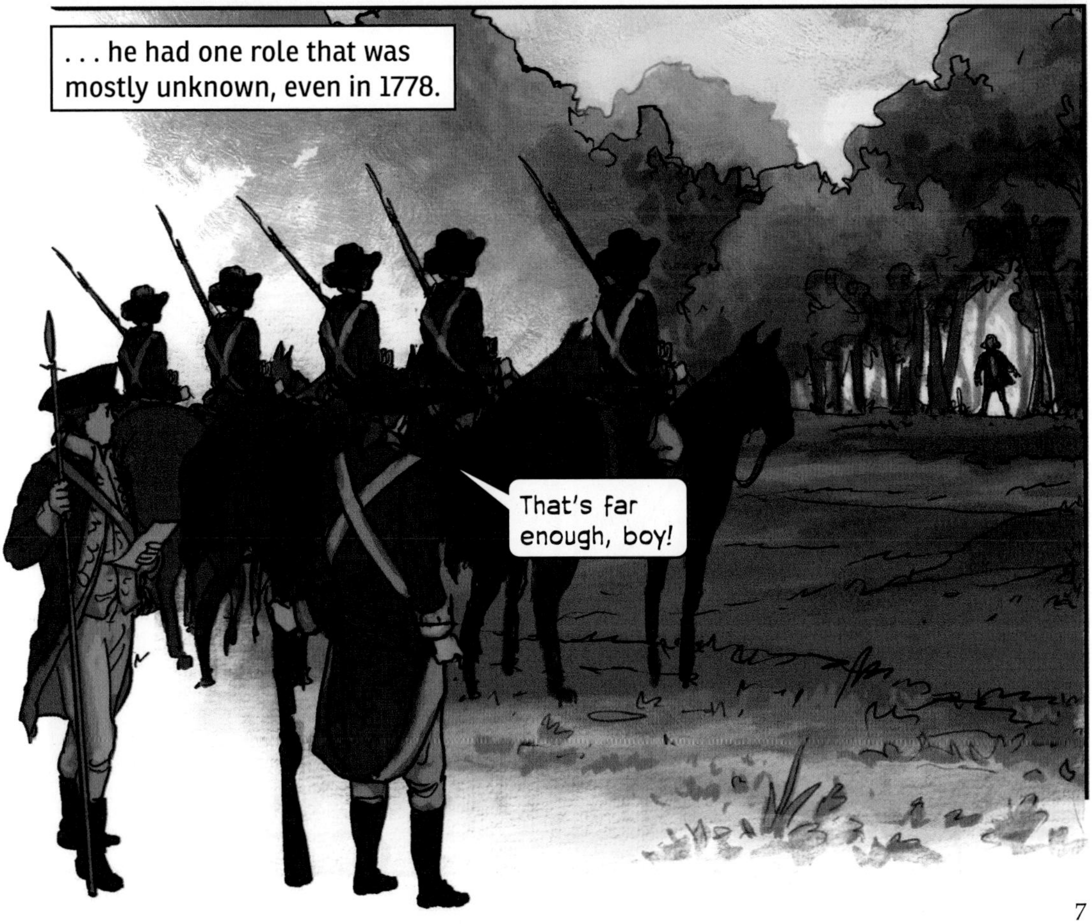
. . . he had one role that was mostly unknown, even in 1778.
That's far enough, boy!

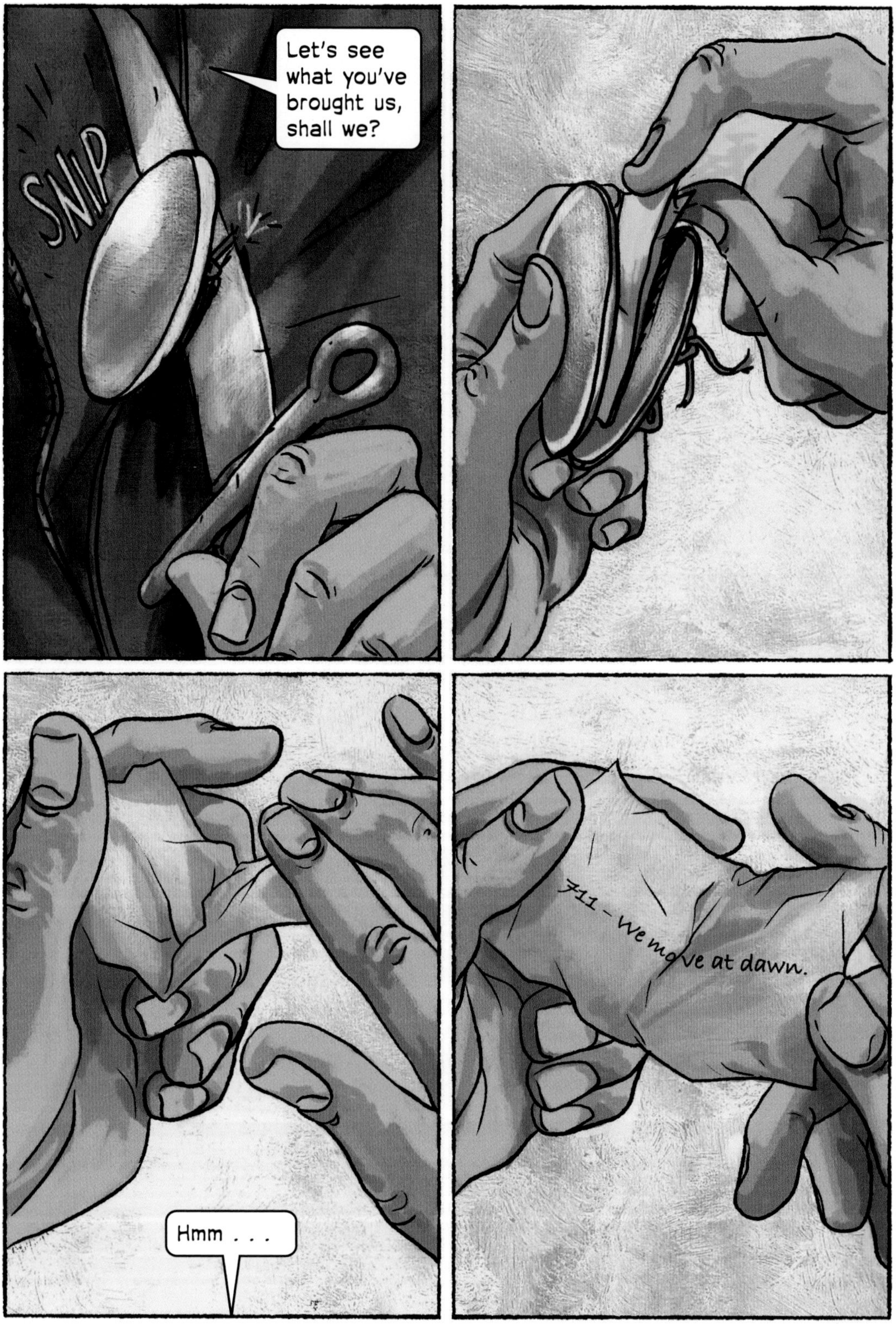
Let's see what you've brought us, shall we?
SNIP
Hmm . . .
711 - We move at dawn.

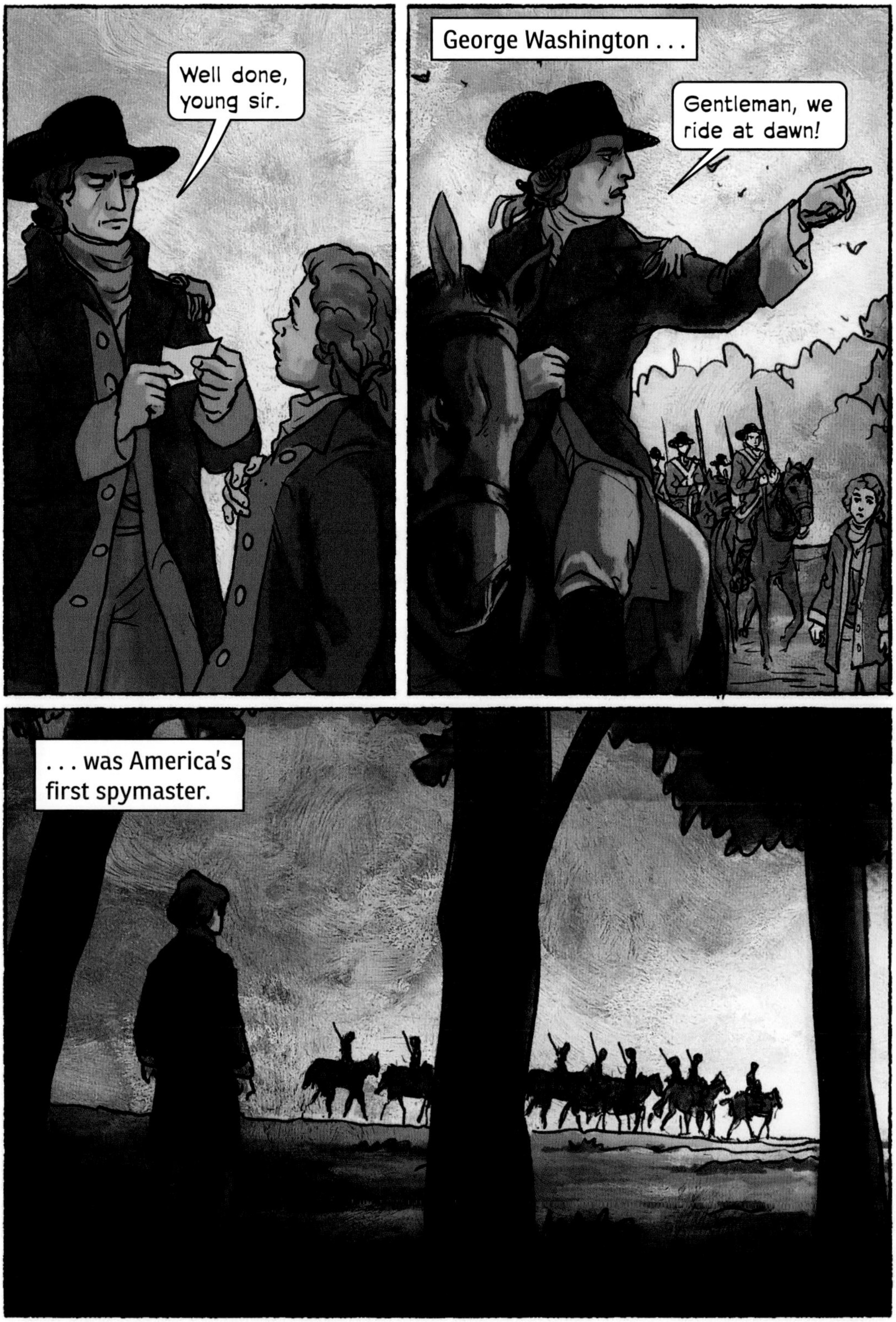
Well done, young sir.
George Washington . . .
Gentleman, we ride at dawn!
. . . was America's first spymaster.

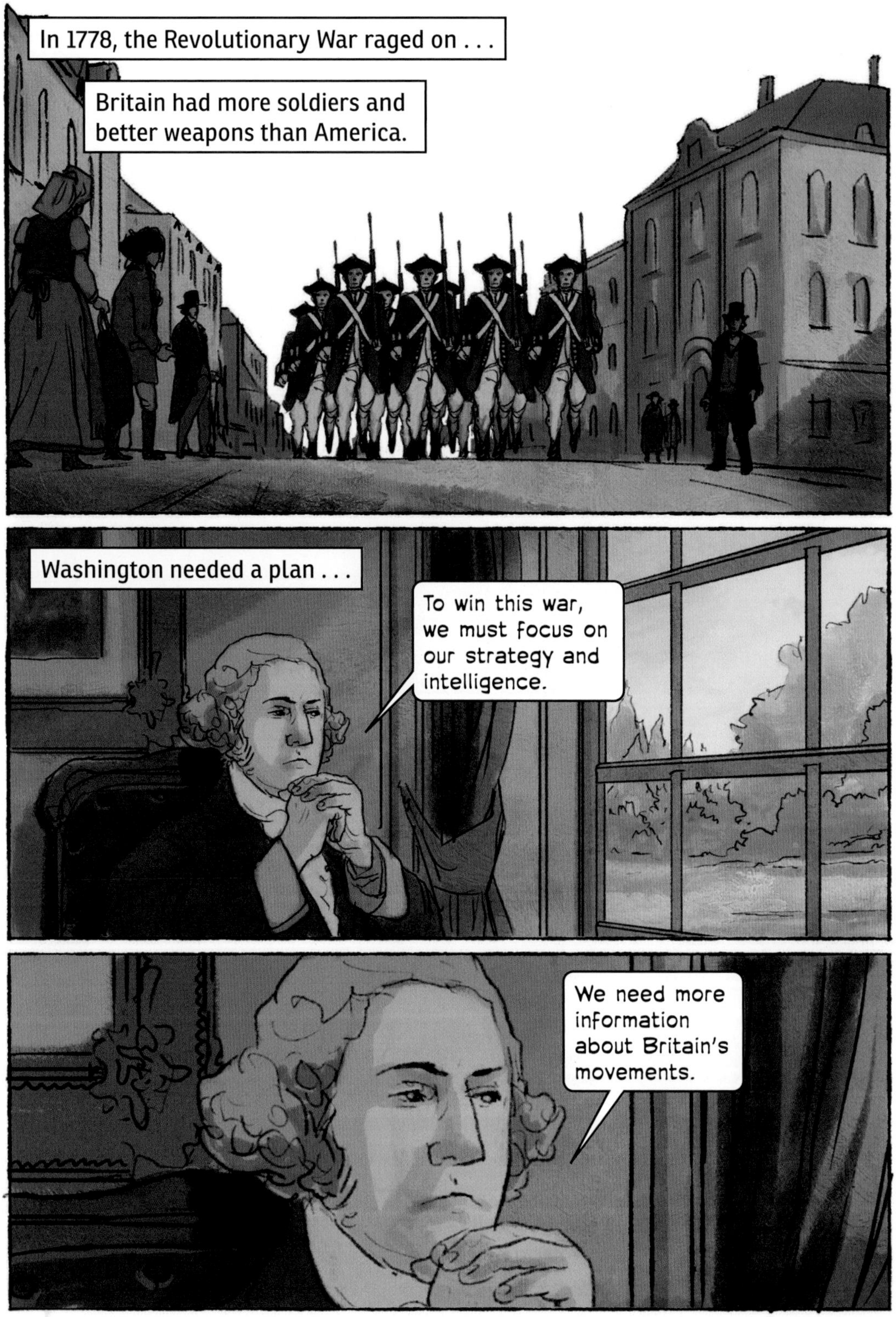
In 1778, the Revolutionary War raged on . . .
Britain had more soldiers and better weapons than America.
Washington needed a plan . . .
To win this war, we must focus on our strategy and intelligence.
We need more information about Britain's movements.

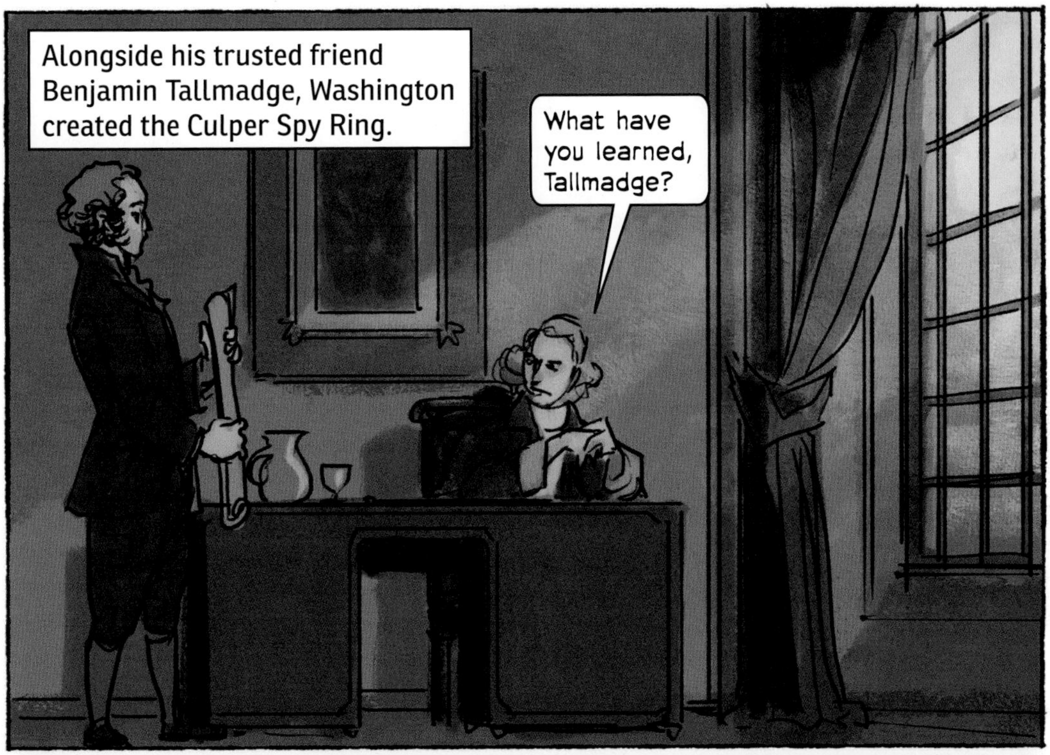
Alongside his trusted friend Benjamin Tallmadge, Washington created the Culper Spy Ring.
What have you learned, Tallmadge?

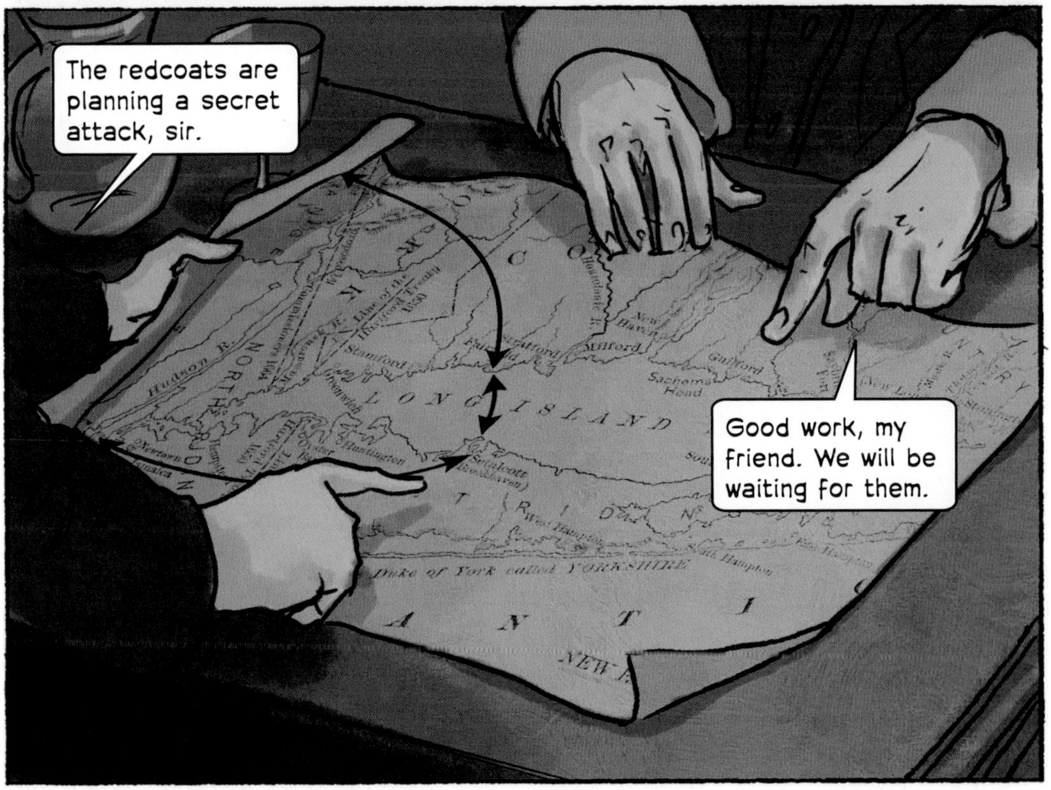
The redcoats are planning a secret attack, sir.
Good work, my friend. We will be waiting for them.
LONG ISLAND
Stamford
Milford
Guilford
Huntington
Duke of York called YORKSHIRE

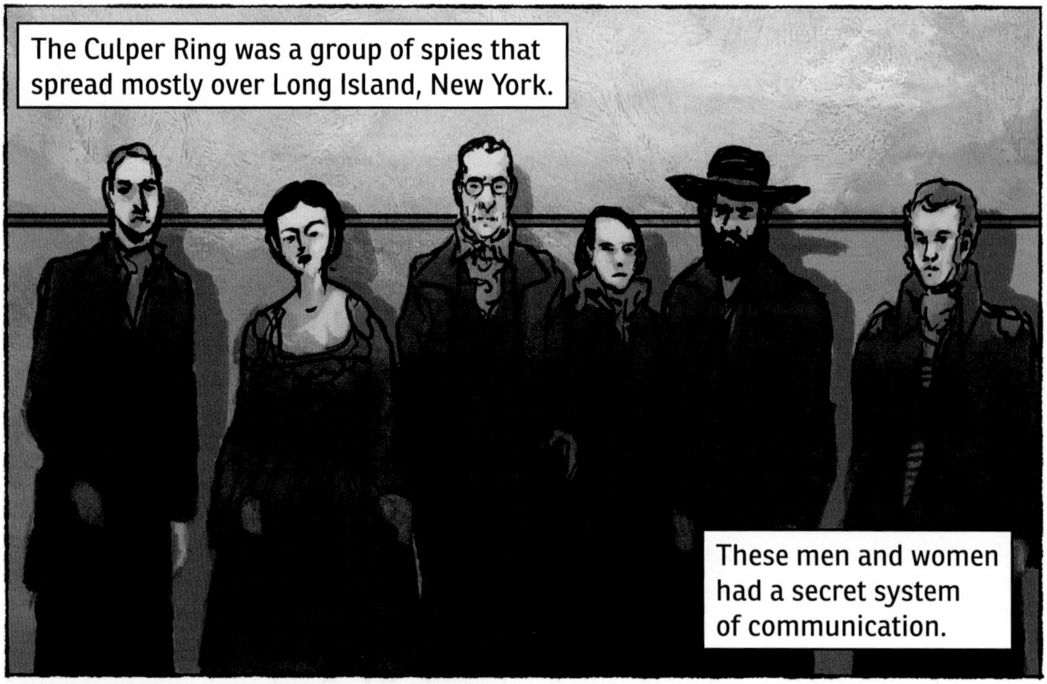
The Culper Ring was a group of spies that spread mostly over Long Island, New York.
These men and women had a secret system of communication.

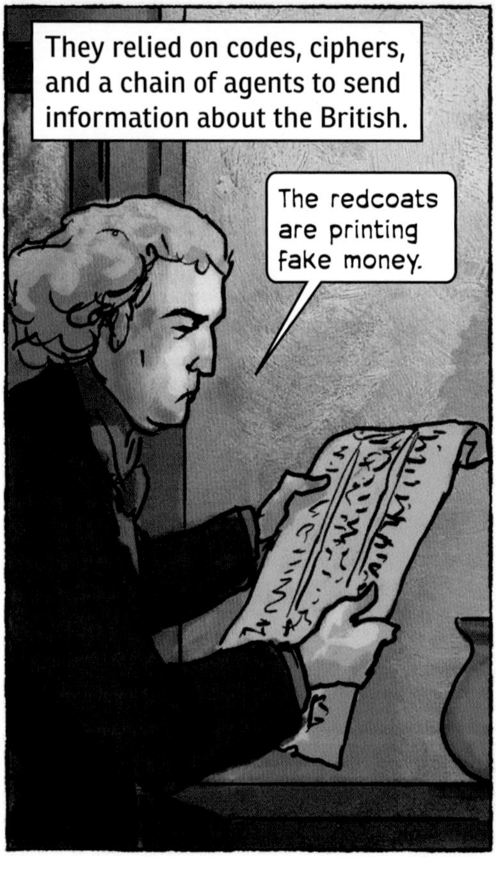
They relied on codes, ciphers, and a chain of agents to send information about the British.
The redcoats are printing fake money.

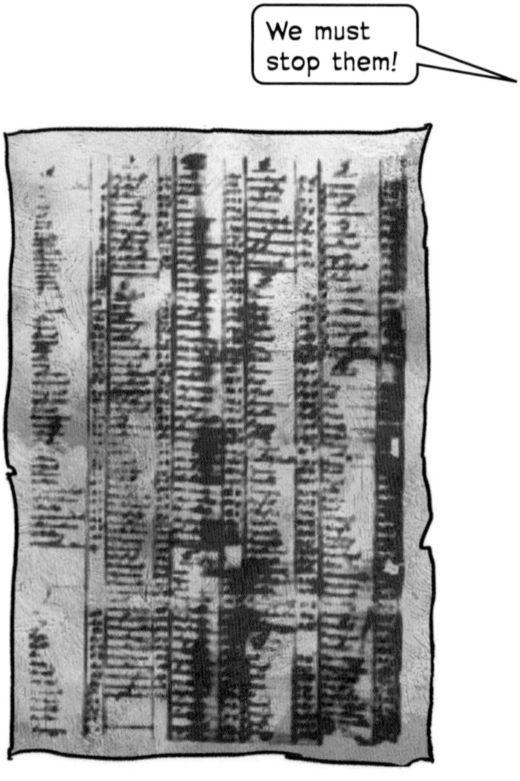
We must stop them!

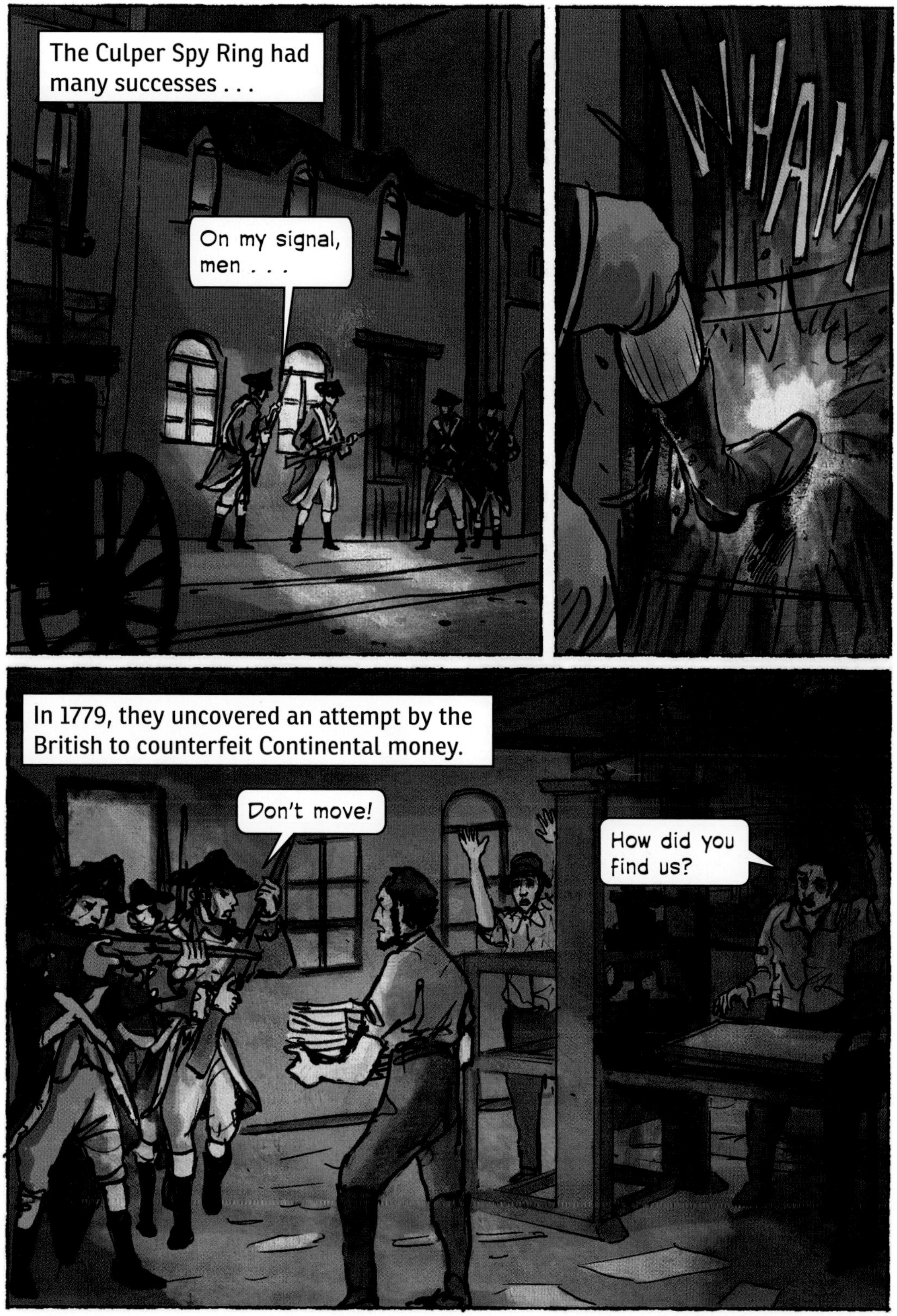
The Culper Spy Ring had many successes . . .
On my signal, men . . .
WHAM
In 1779, they uncovered an attempt by the British to counterfeit Continental money.
Don't move!
How did you find us?

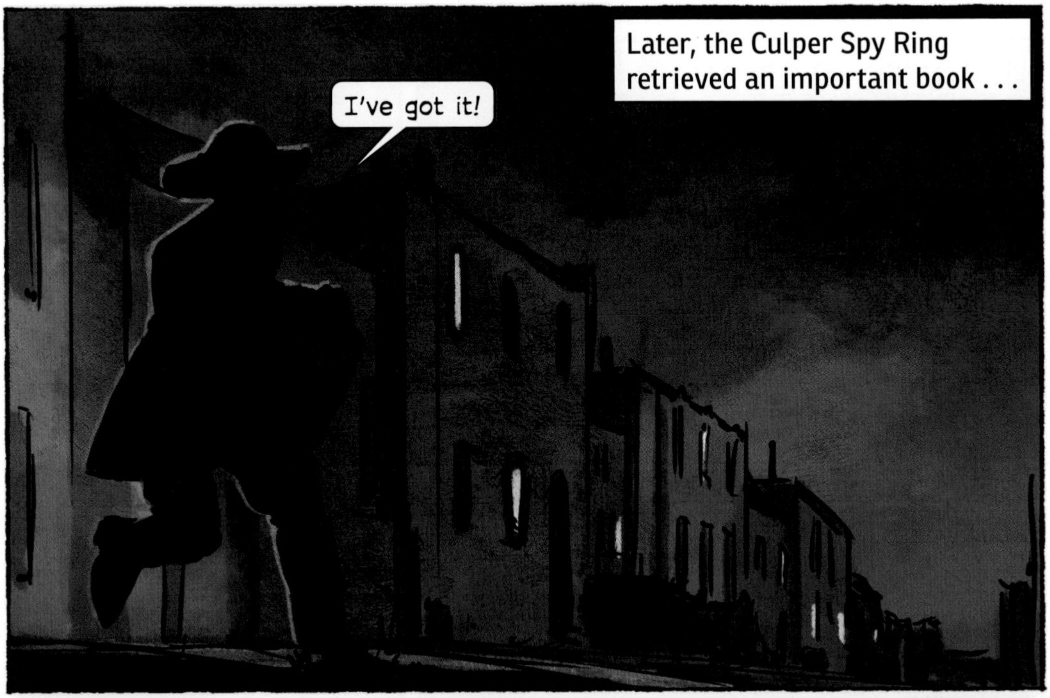
Later, the Culper Spy Ring retrieved an important book . . .
I've got it!

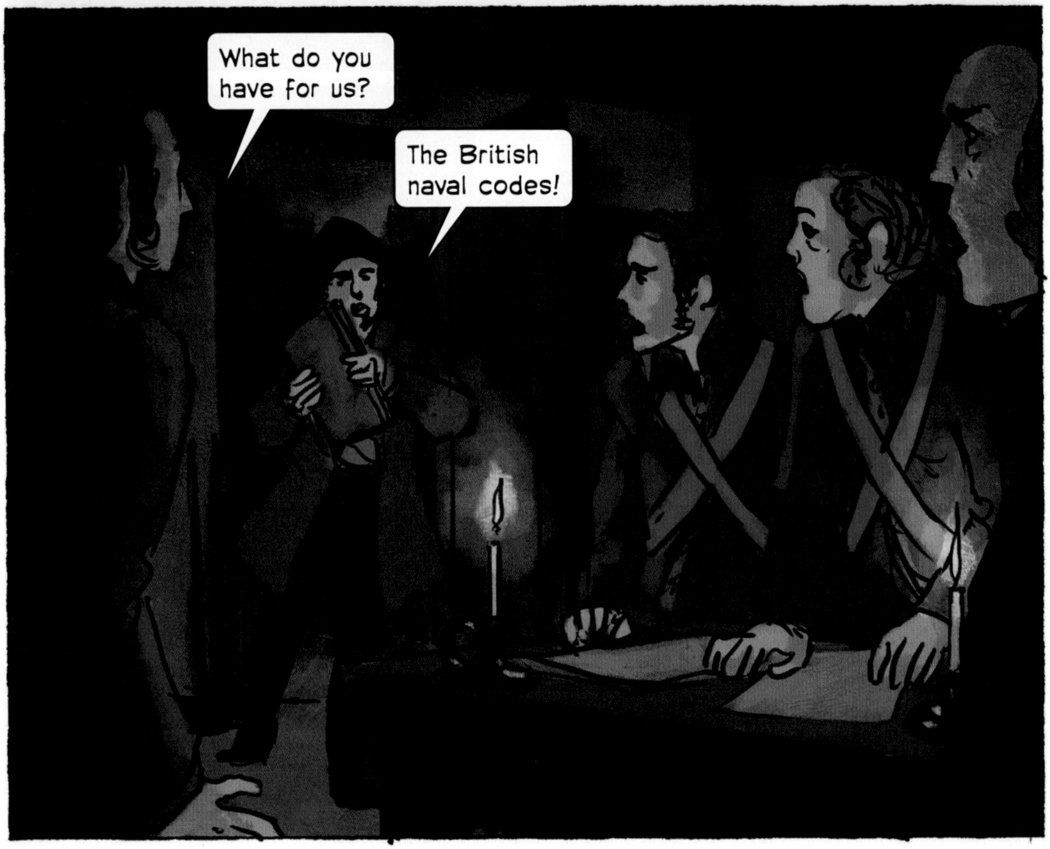
What do you have for us?
The British naval codes!

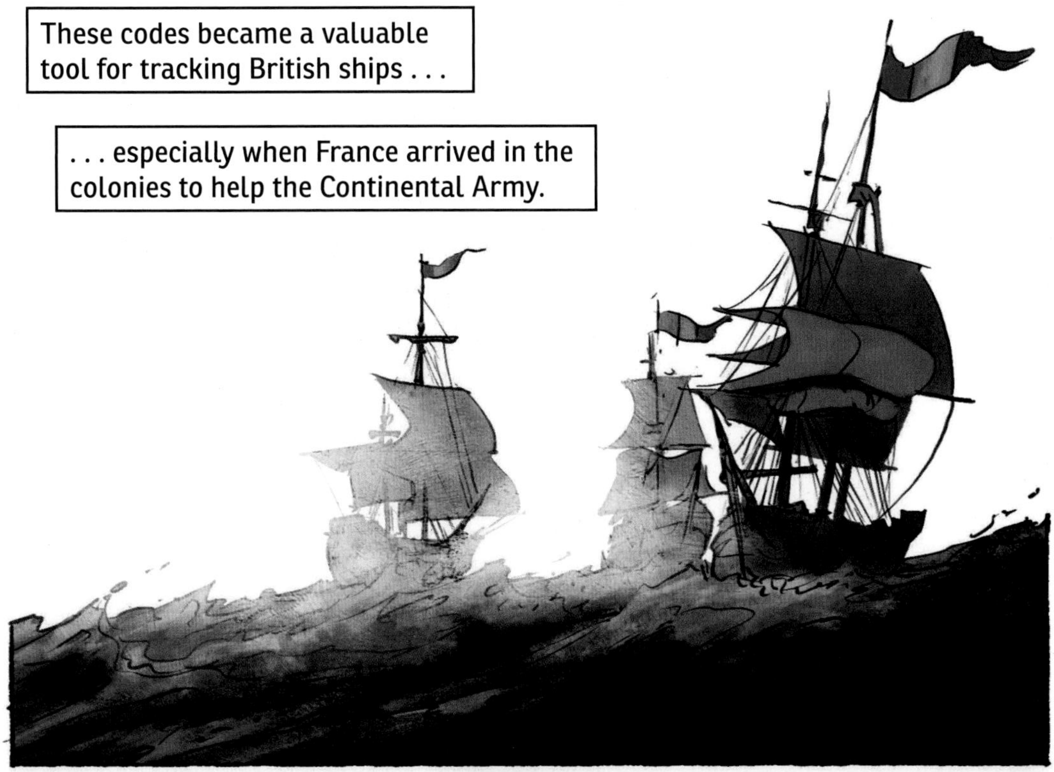
These codes became a valuable tool for tracking British ships . . .
. . . especially when France arrived in the colonies to help the Continental Army.

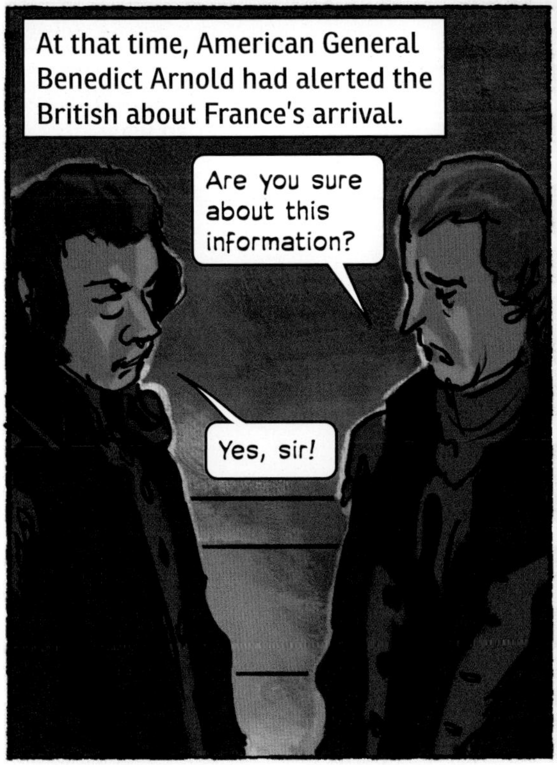
At that time, American General Benedict Arnold had alerted the British about France's arrival.
Are you sure about this information?
Yes, sir!

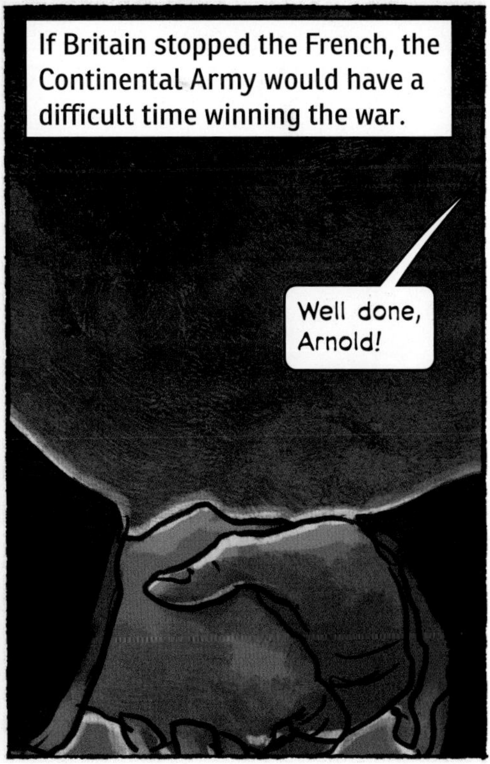
If Britain stopped the French, the Continental Army would have a difficult time winning the war.
Well done, Arnold!

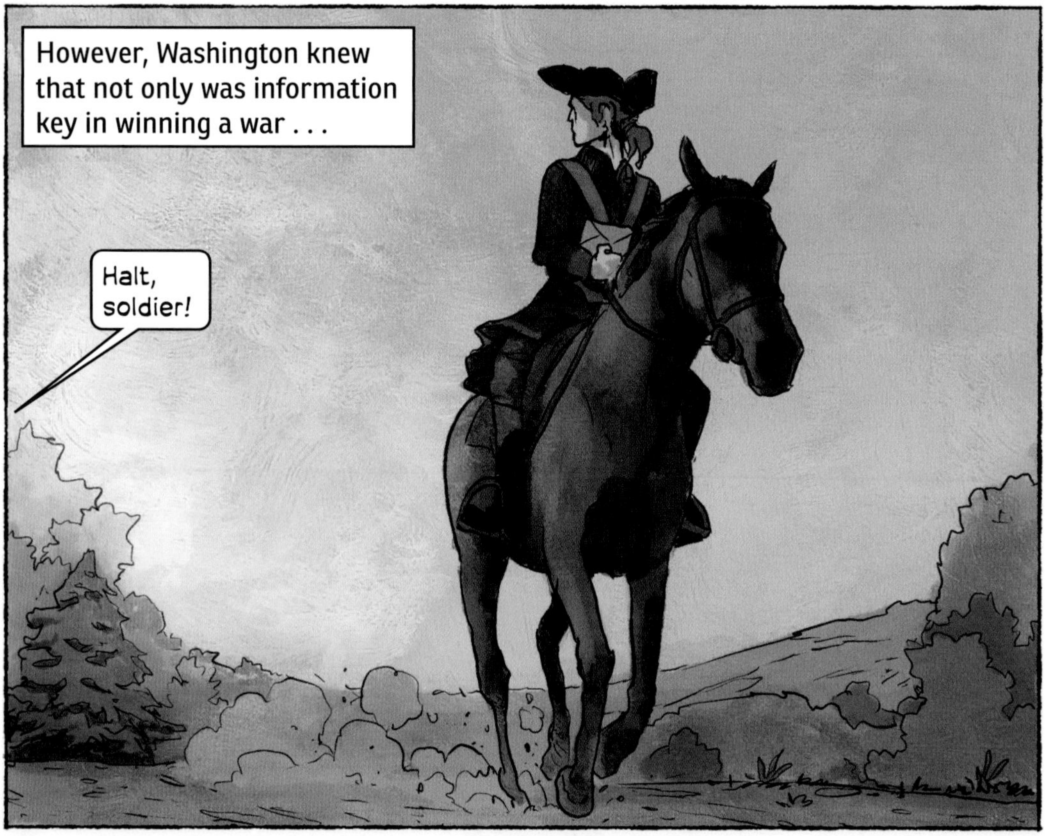
However, Washington knew that not only was information key in winning a war . . .
Halt, soldier!

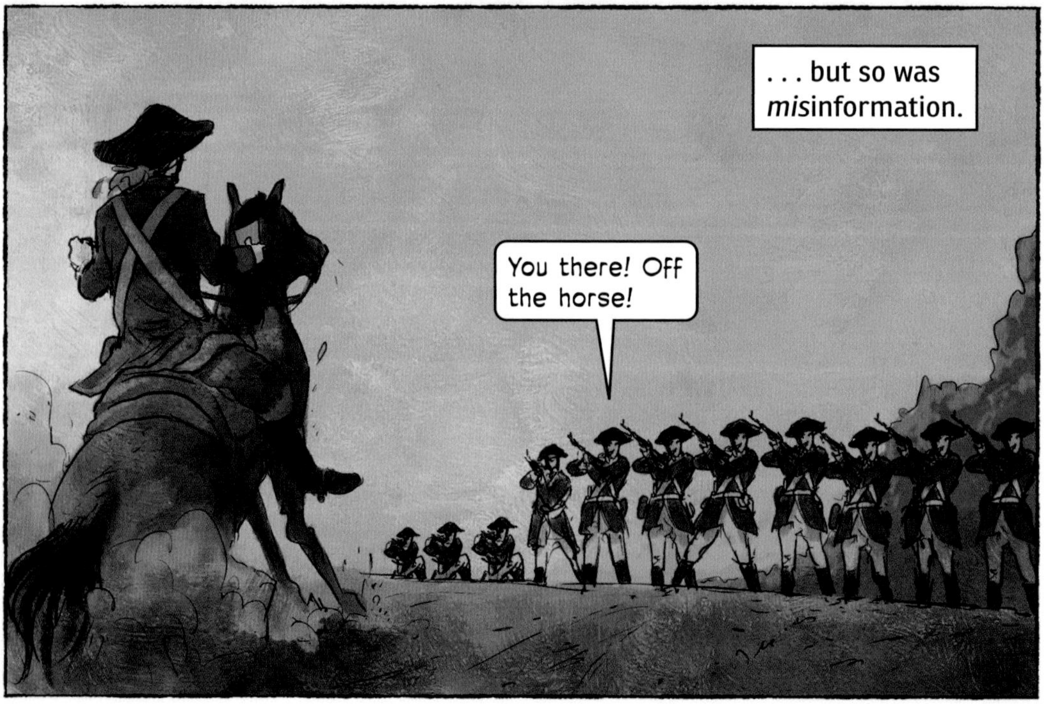
. . . but so was *mis*information.
You there! Off the horse!

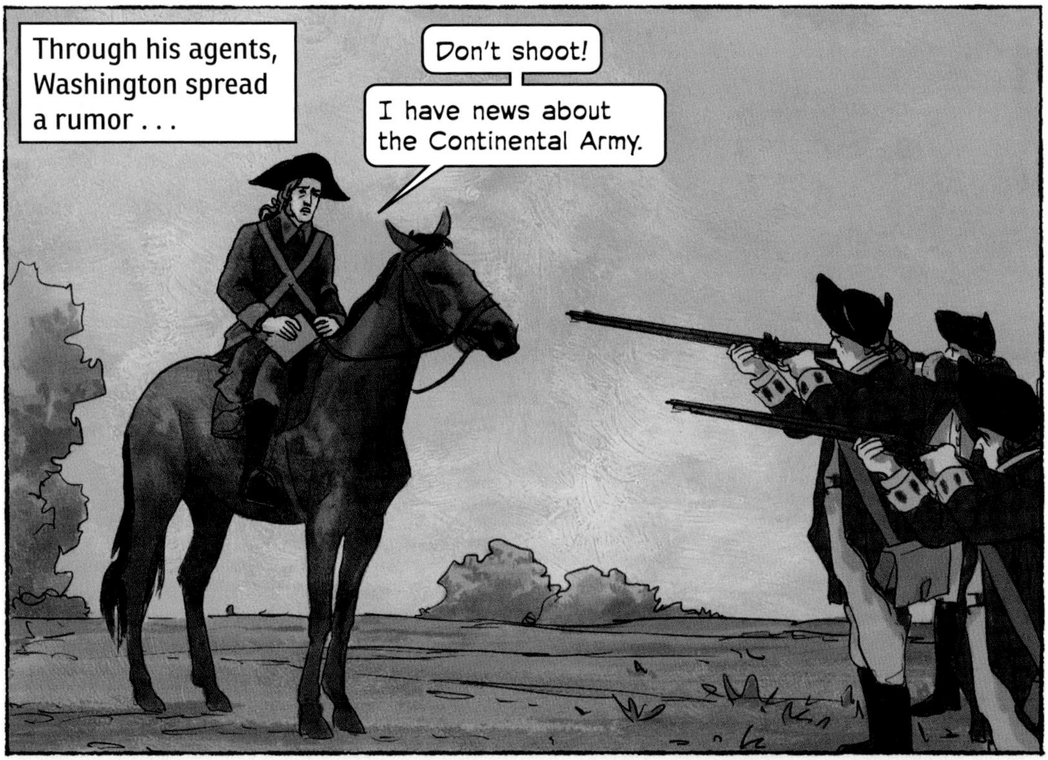
Through his agents, Washington spread a rumor . . .
Don't shoot!
I have news about the Continental Army.

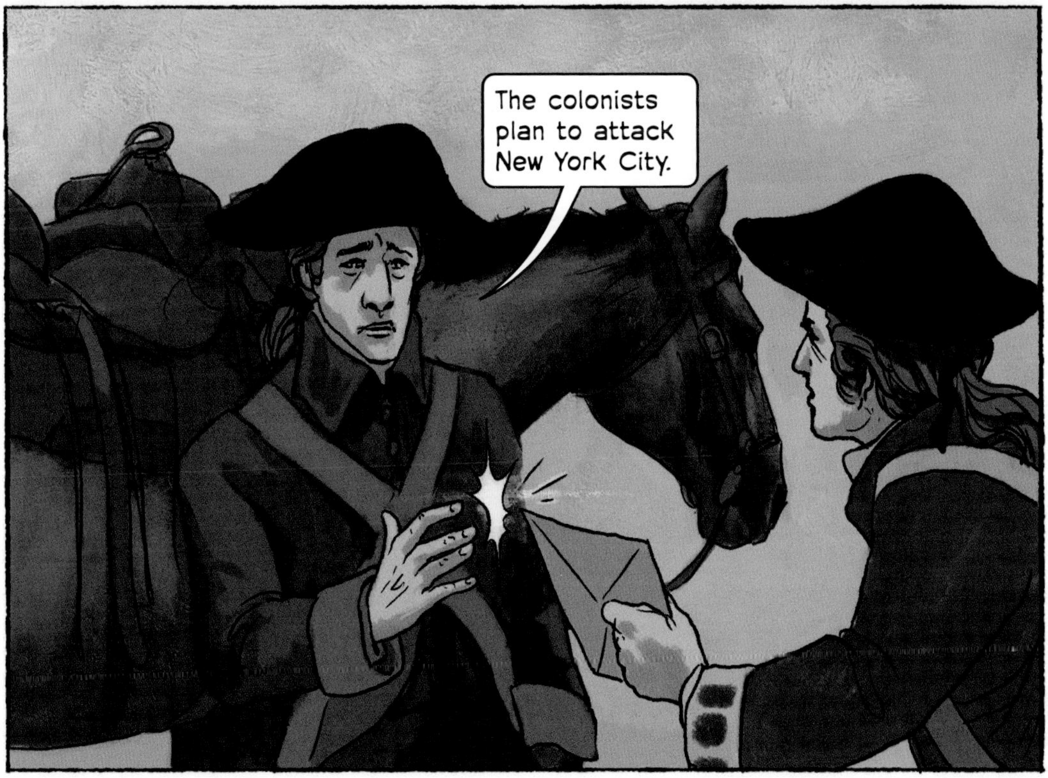
The colonists plan to attack New York City.

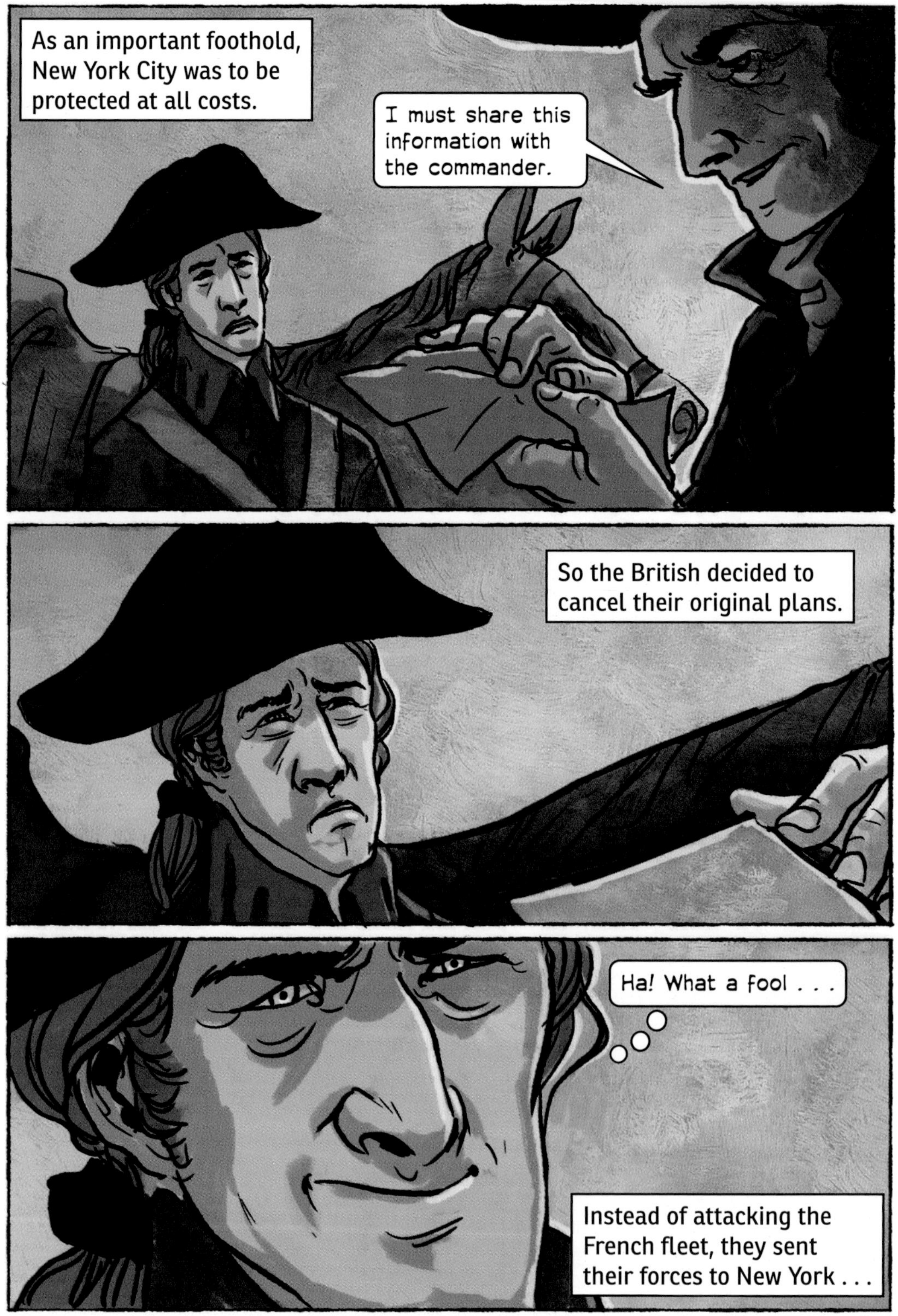
As an important foothold, New York City was to be protected at all costs.
I must share this information with the commander.
So the British decided to cancel their original plans.
Ha! What a fool . . .
Instead of attacking the French fleet, they sent their forces to New York . . .

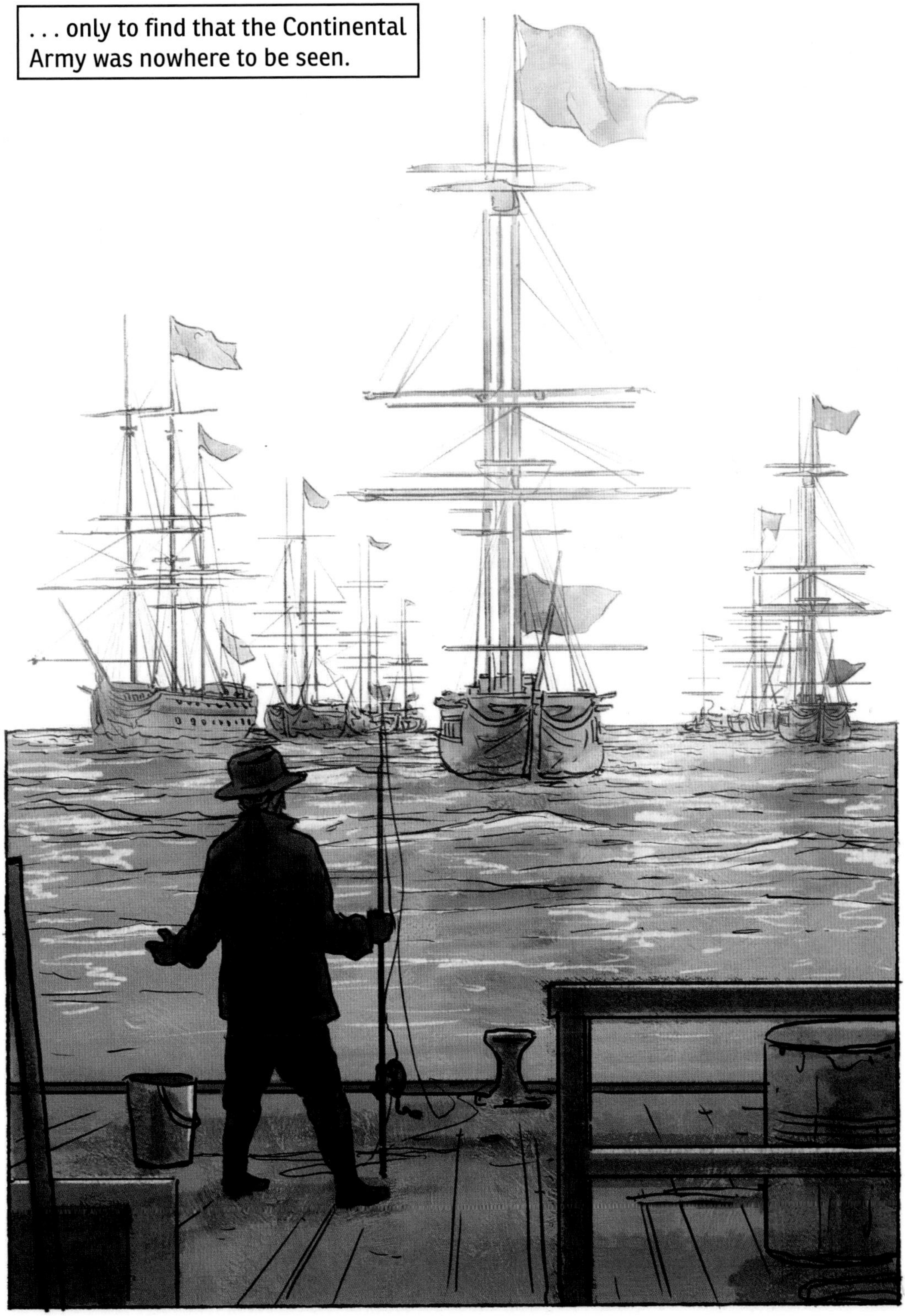
. . . only to find that the Continental Army was nowhere to be seen.

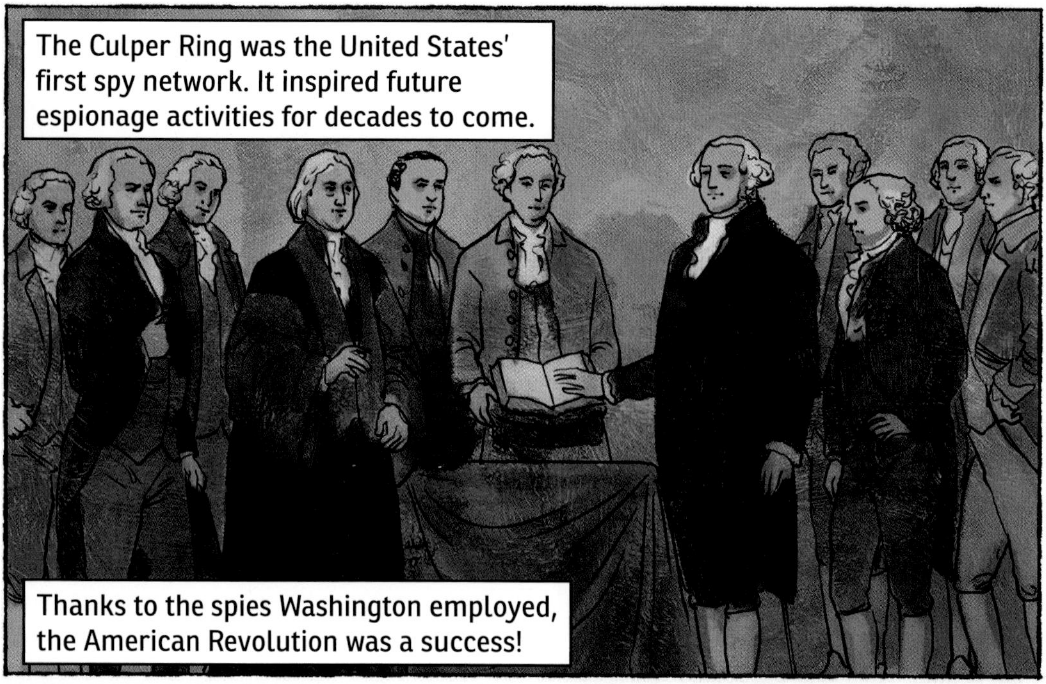
The Culper Ring was the United States' first spy network. It inspired future espionage activities for decades to come.
Thanks to the spies Washington employed, the American Revolution was a success!

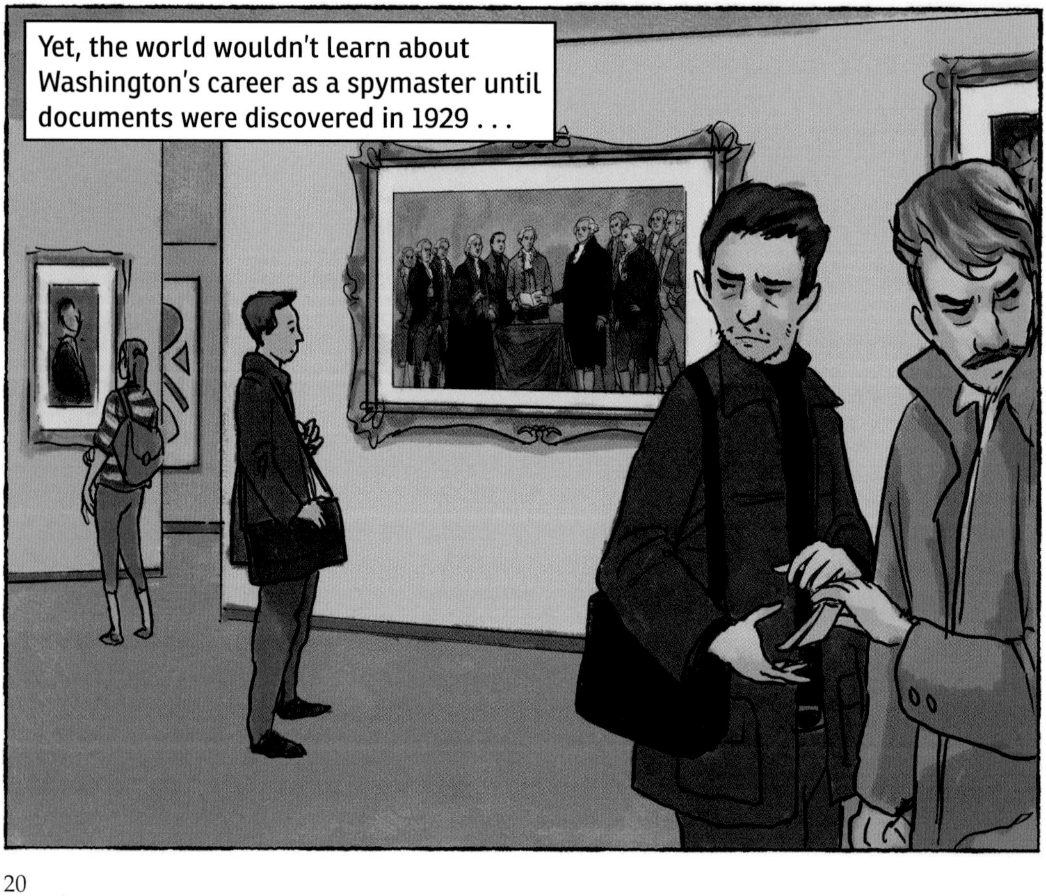
Yet, the world wouldn't learn about Washington's career as a spymaster until documents were discovered in 1929 . . .

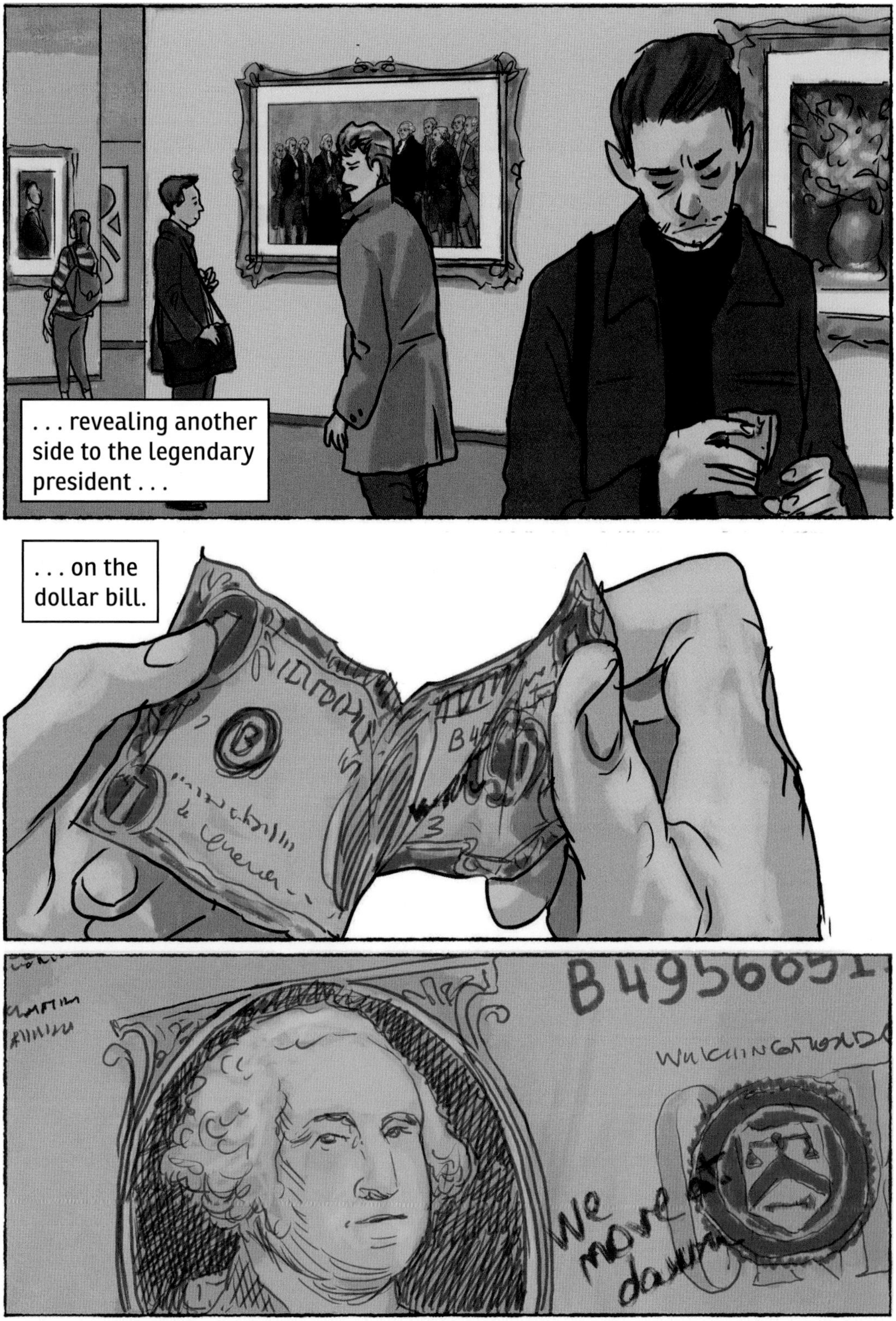
. . . revealing another side to the legendary president . . .
. . . on the dollar bill.
We move at dawn

CHAPTER TWO

BENJAMIN TALLMADGE: THE SILENT SPY

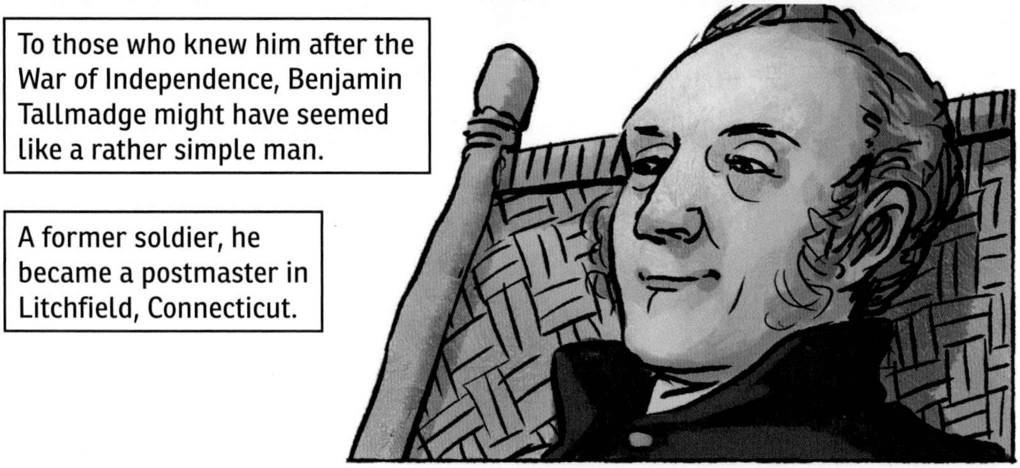
To those who knew him after the War of Independence, Benjamin Tallmadge might have seemed like a rather simple man.
A former soldier, he became a postmaster in Litchfield, Connecticut.

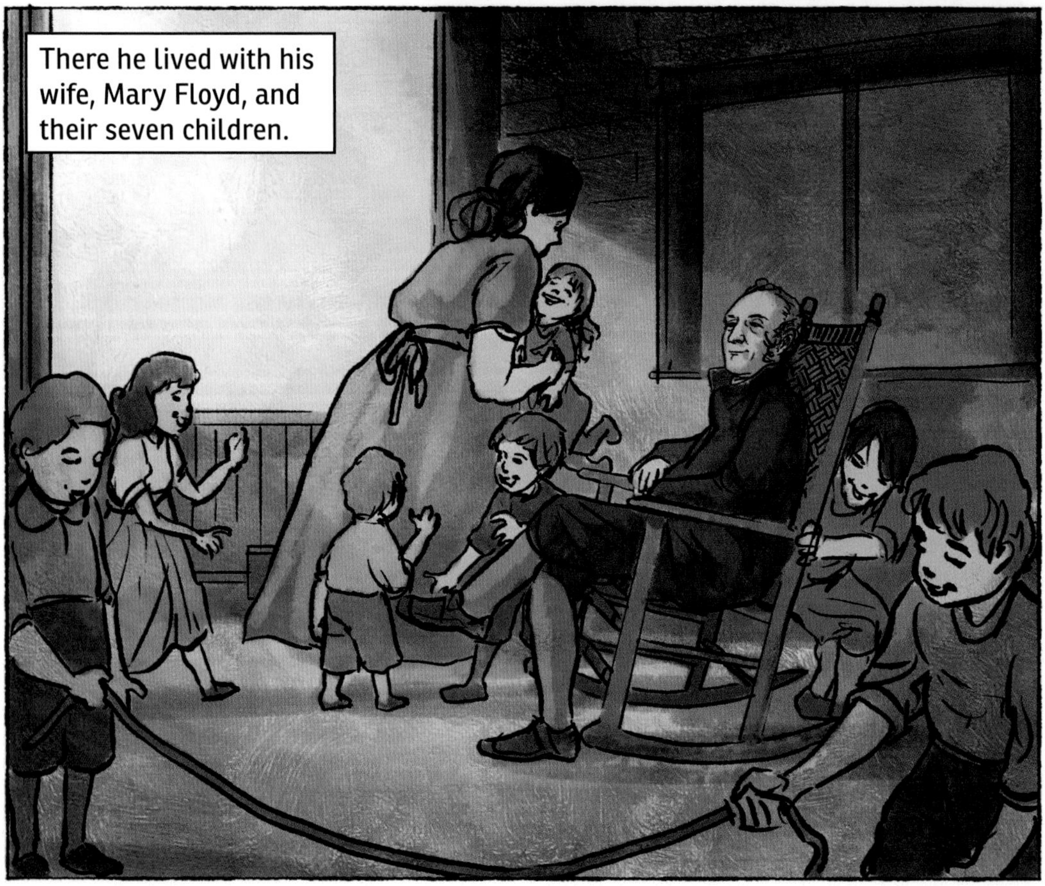
There he lived with his wife, Mary Floyd, and their seven children.

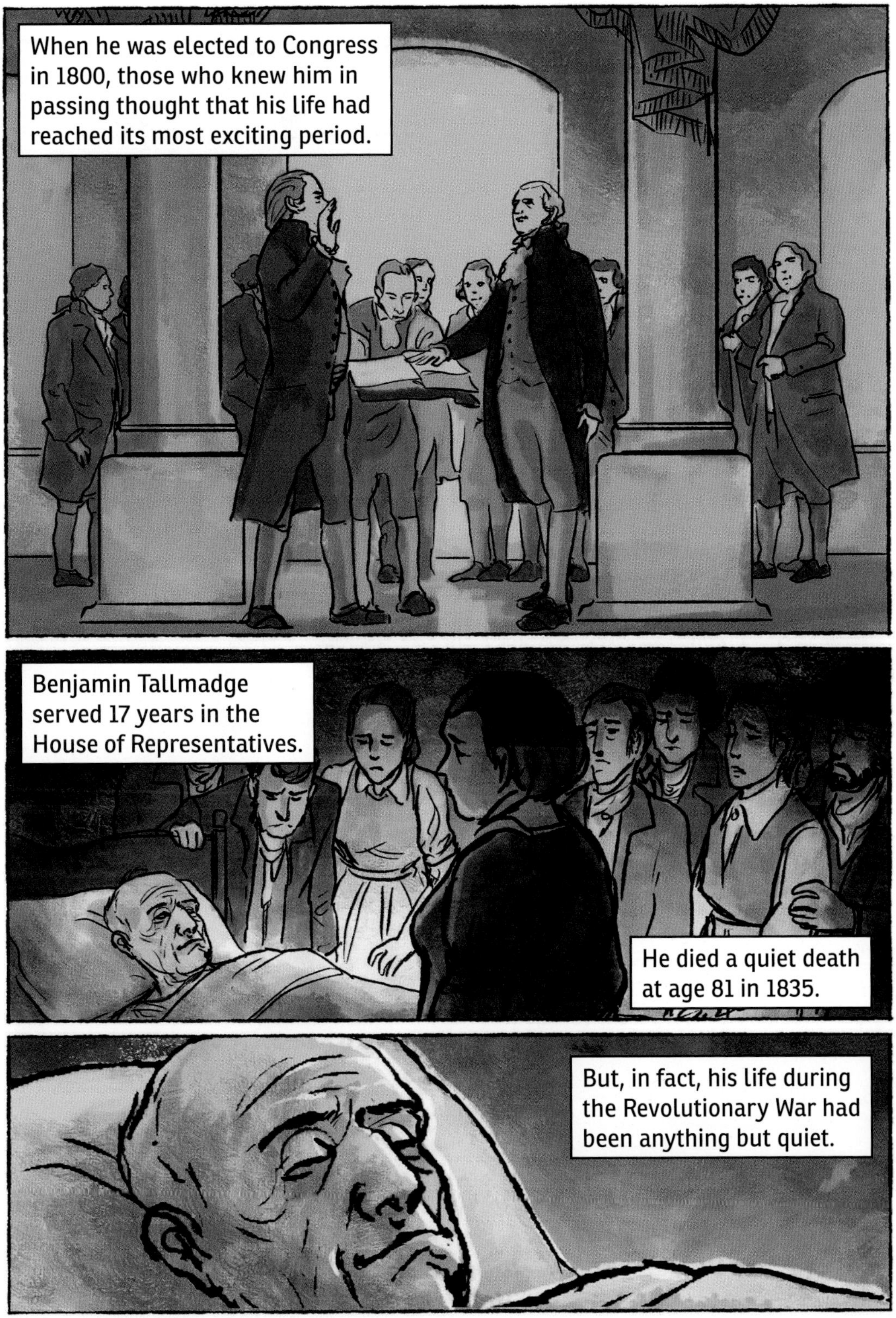
When he was elected to Congress in 1800, those who knew him in passing thought that his life had reached its most exciting period.
Benjamin Tallmadge served 17 years in the House of Representatives.
He died a quiet death at age 81 in 1835.
But, in fact, his life during the Revolutionary War had been anything but quiet.

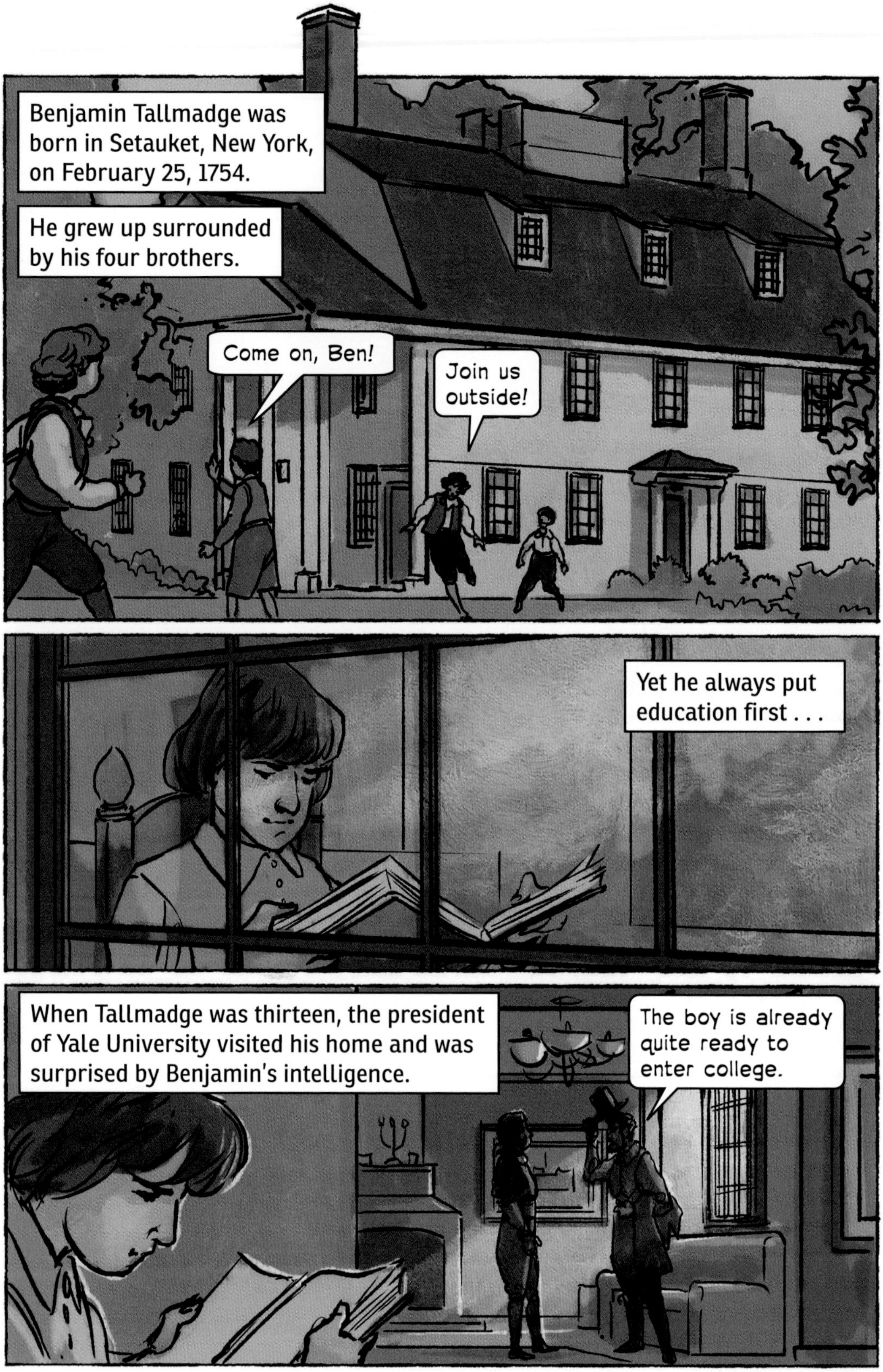
Benjamin Tallmadge was born in Setauket, New York, on February 25, 1754.
He grew up surrounded by his four brothers.
Come on, Ben!
Join us outside!
Yet he always put education first . . .
When Tallmadge was thirteen, the president of Yale University visited his home and was surprised by Benjamin's intelligence.
The boy is already quite ready to enter college.

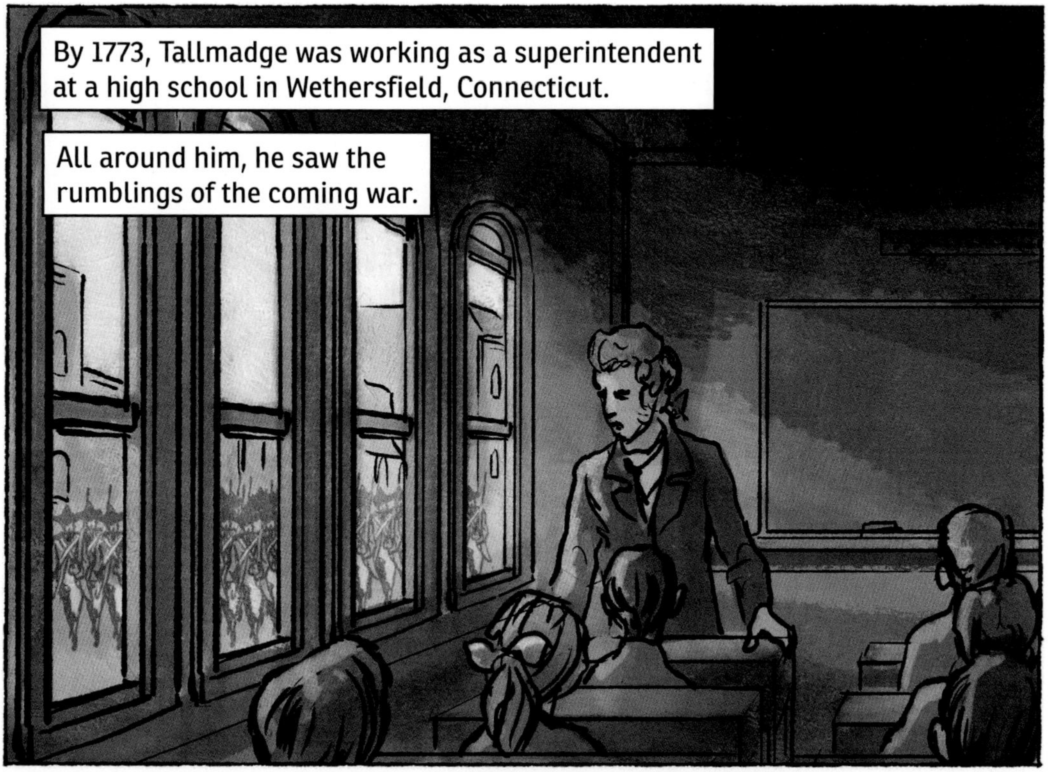
By 1773, Tallmadge was working as a superintendent at a high school in Wethersfield, Connecticut.
All around him, he saw the rumblings of the coming war.

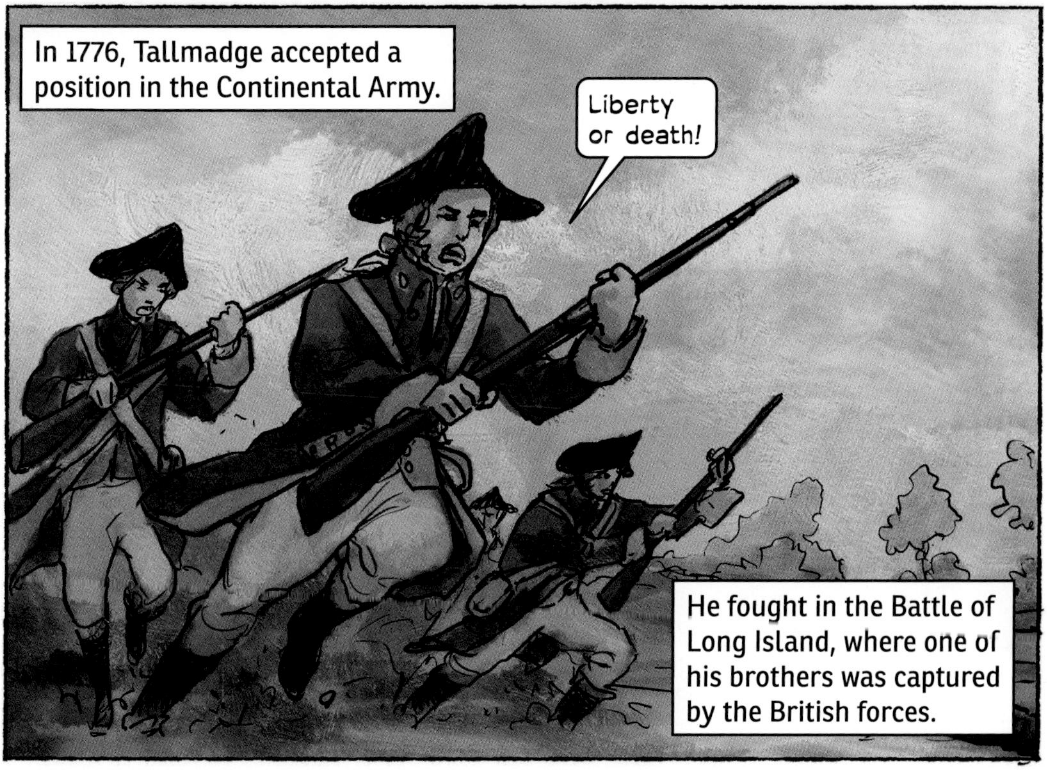
In 1776, Tallmadge accepted a position in the Continental Army.
Liberty or death!
He fought in the Battle of Long Island, where one of his brothers was captured by the British forces.

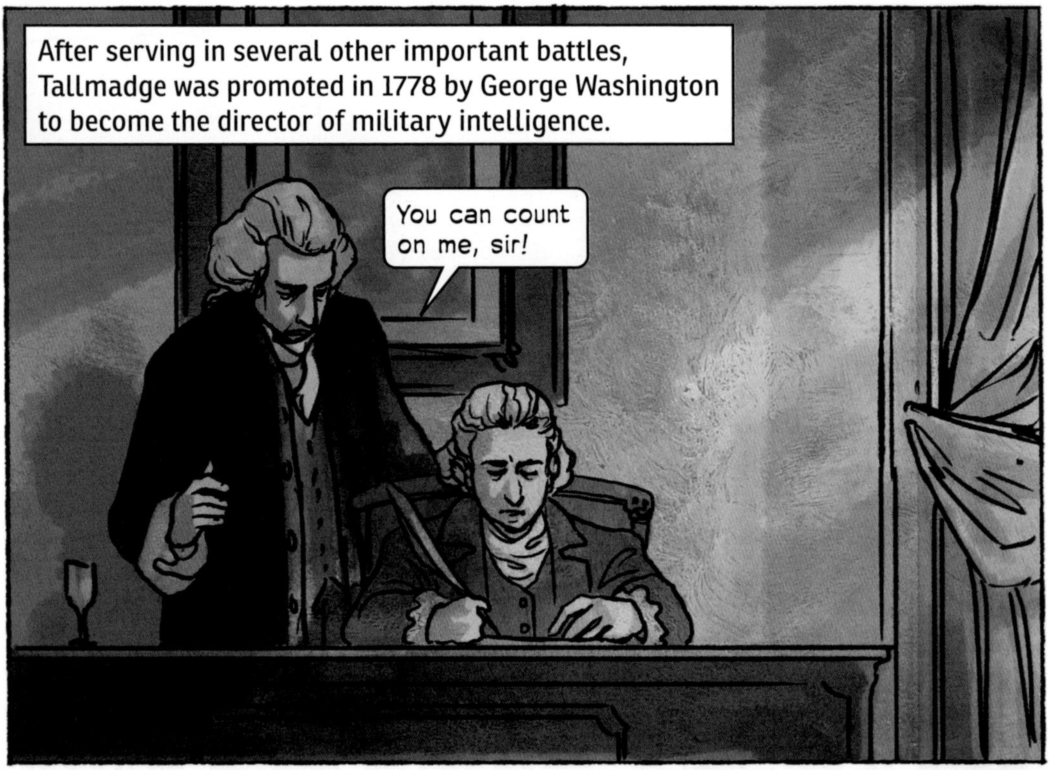
After serving in several other important battles, Tallmadge was promoted in 1778 by George Washington to become the director of military intelligence.
You can count on me, sir!

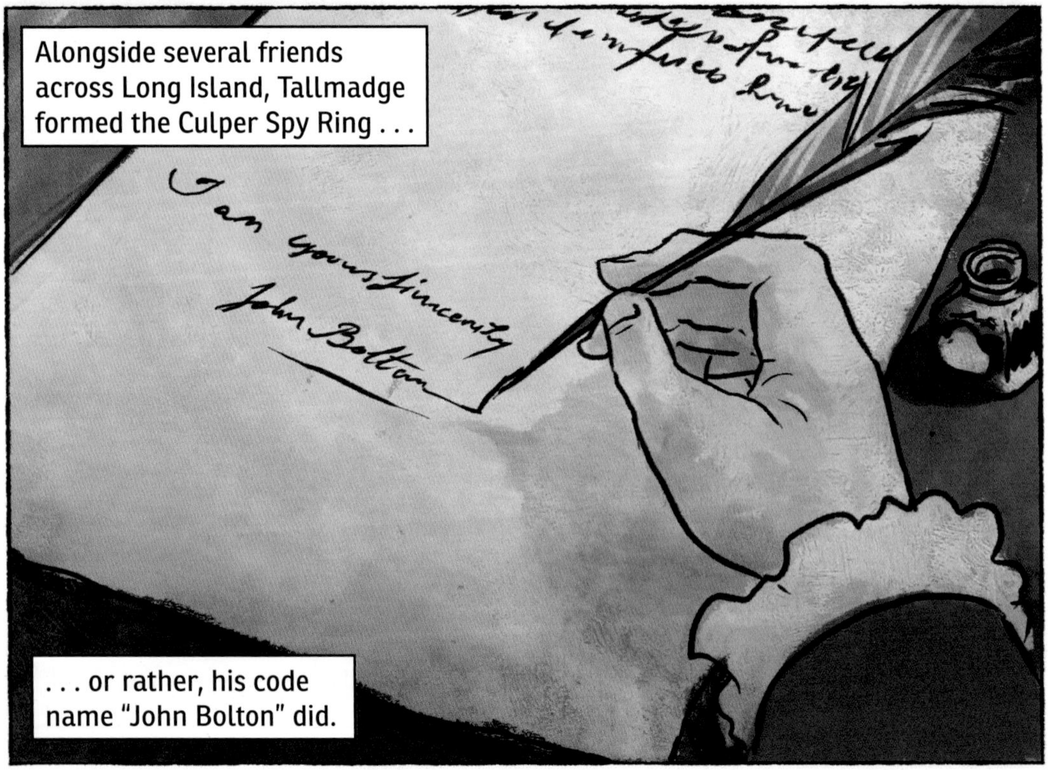
Alongside several friends across Long Island, Tallmadge formed the Culper Spy Ring . . .
I am yours sincerely
John Bolton
. . . or rather, his code name "John Bolton" did.

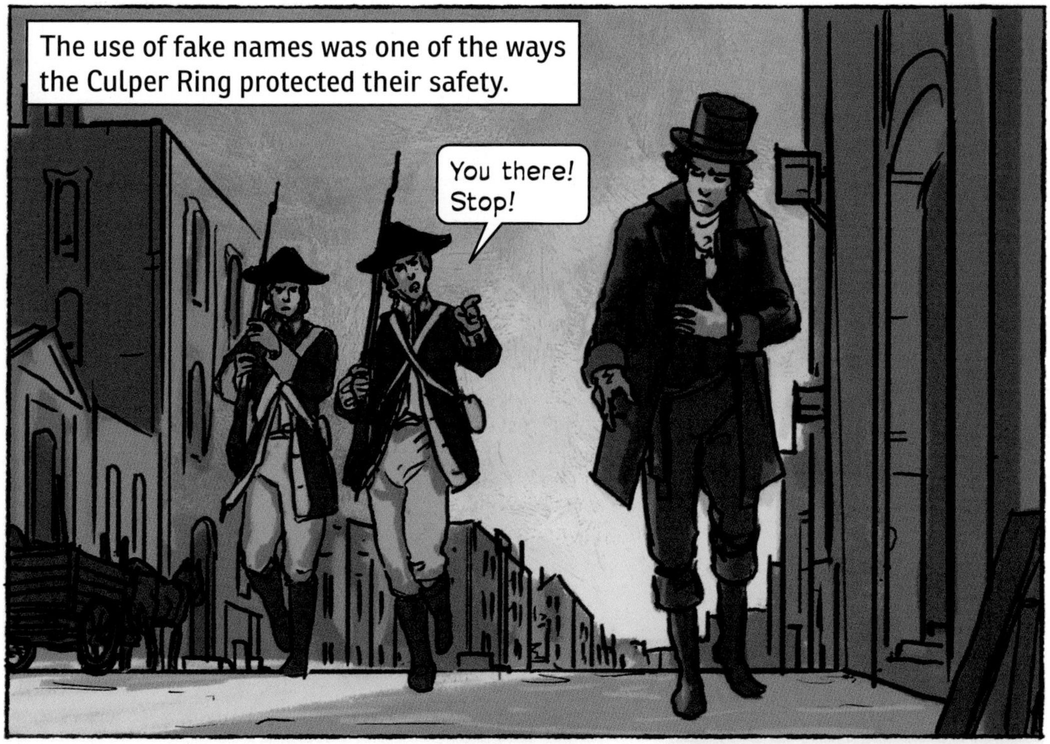
The use of fake names was one of the ways the Culper Ring protected their safety.
You there! Stop!

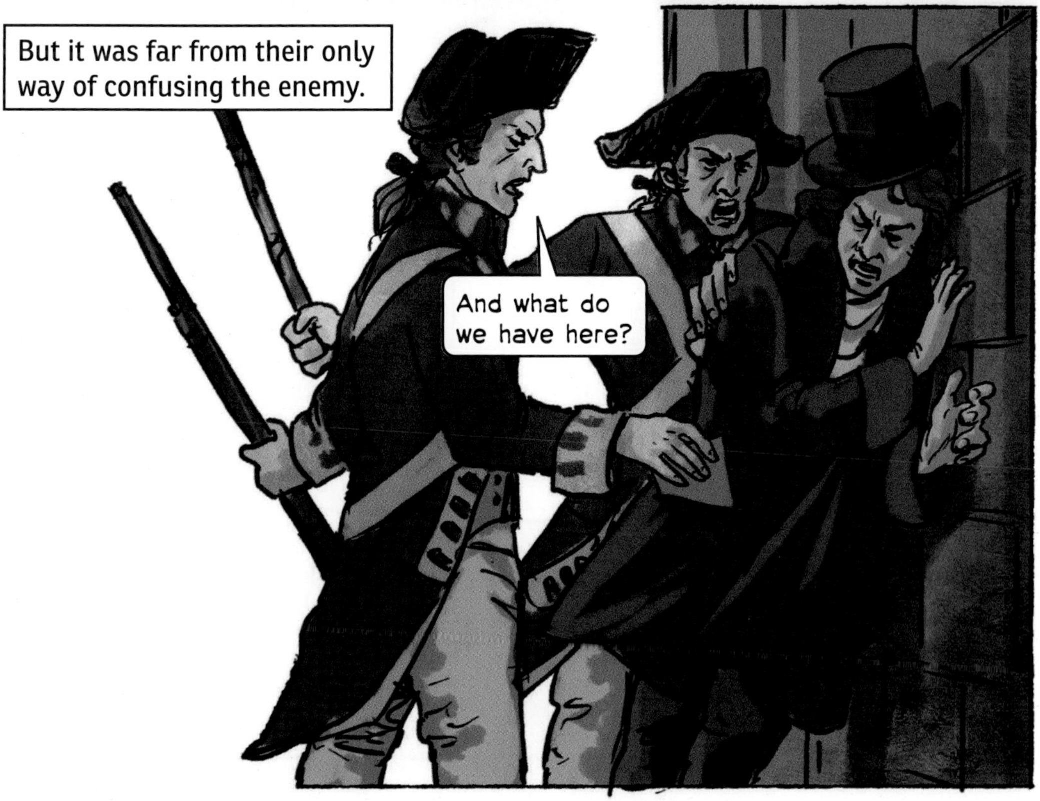
But it was far from their only way of confusing the enemy.
And what do we have here?

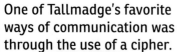

One of Tallmadge's favorite ways of communication was through the use of a cipher.

He and Washington devised a codebook where numbers stood for various people, locations, and common words.

What is this? It's nothing more than a bunch of numbers!

For example, the number 711 stood for George Washington himself.

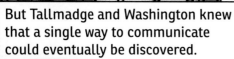

But Tallmadge and Washington knew that a single way to communicate could eventually be discovered.

What if we came up with an ink that would only appear when wiped with another liquid?

So Washington came up with another idea.

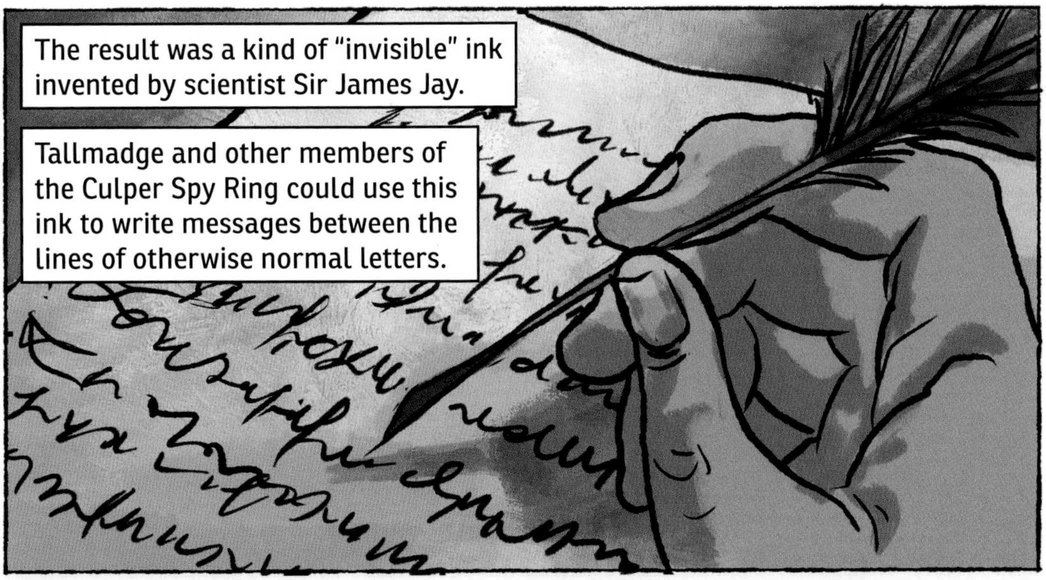
The result was a kind of "invisible" ink invented by scientist Sir James Jay.
Tallmadge and other members of the Culper Spy Ring could use this ink to write messages between the lines of otherwise normal letters.

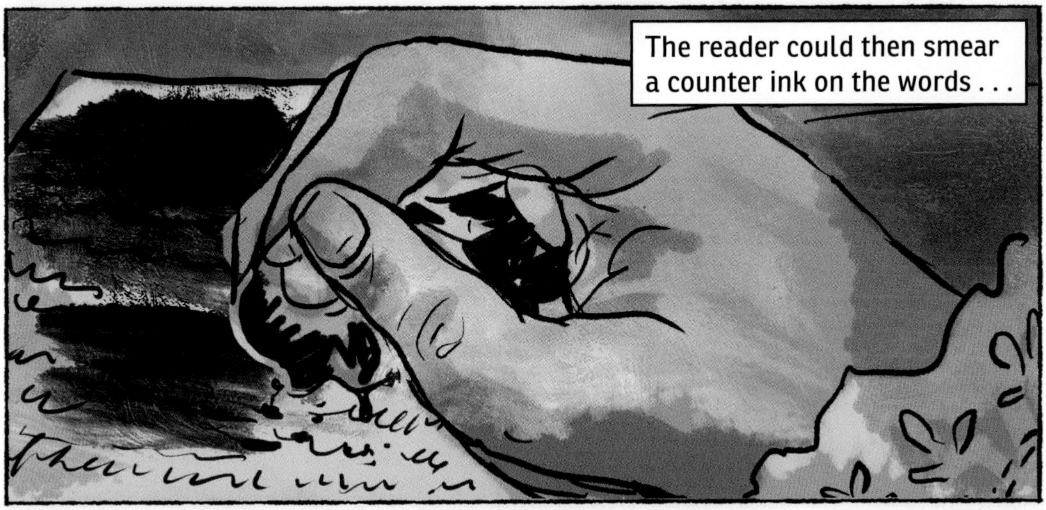
The reader could then smear a counter ink on the words . . .

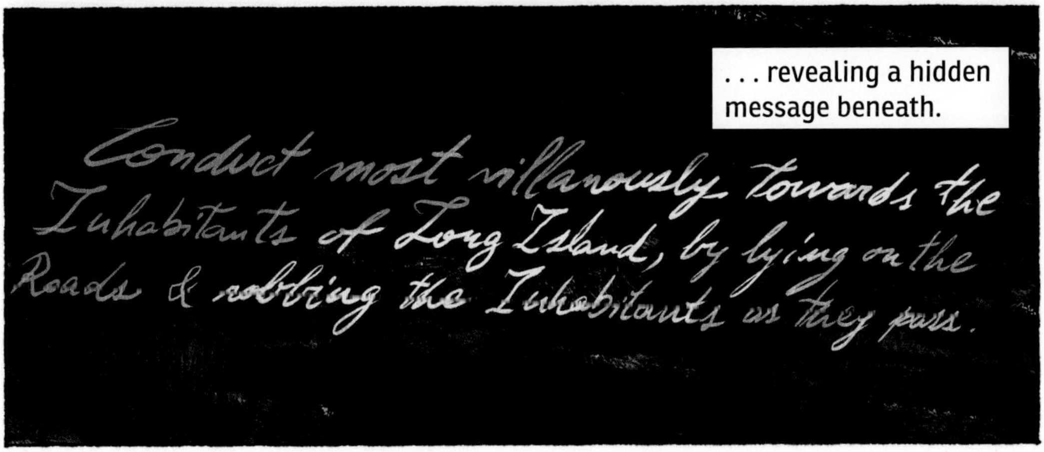
. . . revealing a hidden message beneath.
Conduct most villanously towards the Inhabitants of Long Island, by lying on the Roads & robbing the Inhabitants as they pass.

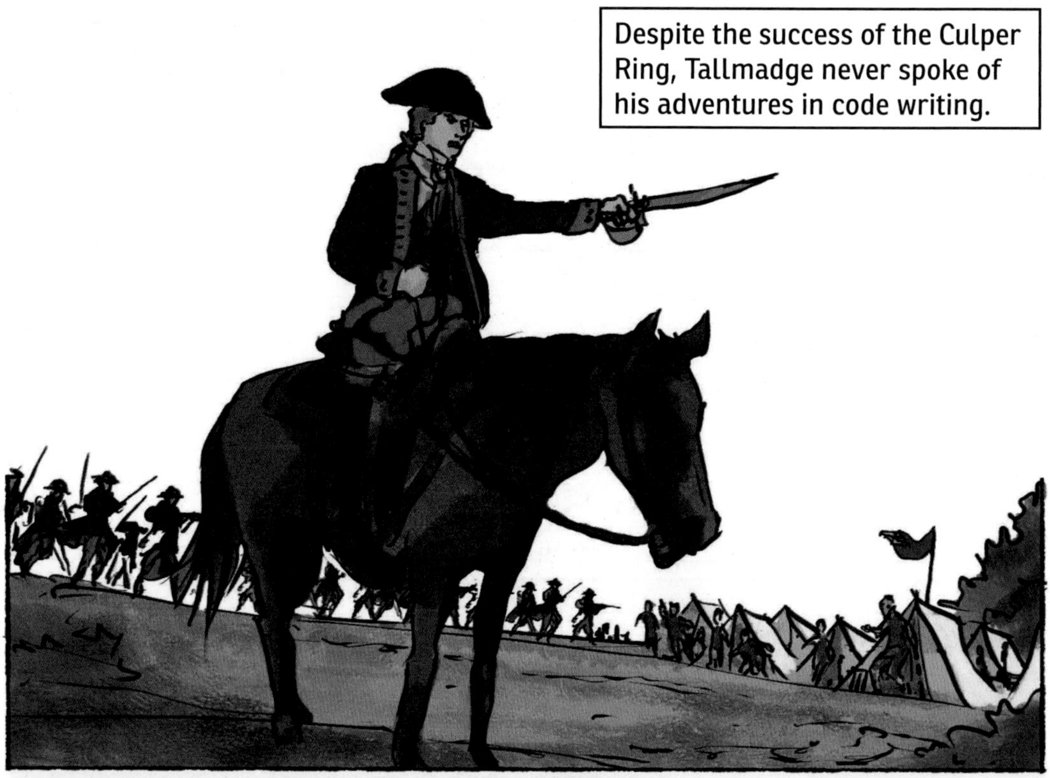
Despite the success of the Culper Ring, Tallmadge never spoke of his adventures in code writing.

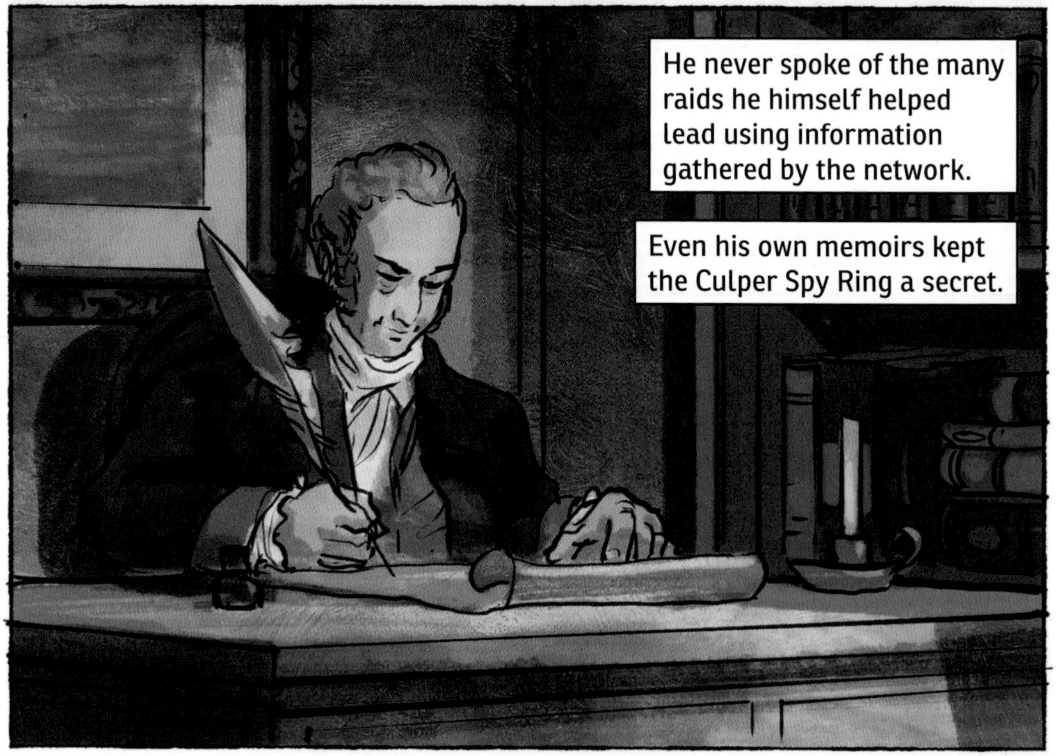
He never spoke of the many raids he himself helped lead using information gathered by the network.
Even his own memoirs kept the Culper Spy Ring a secret.

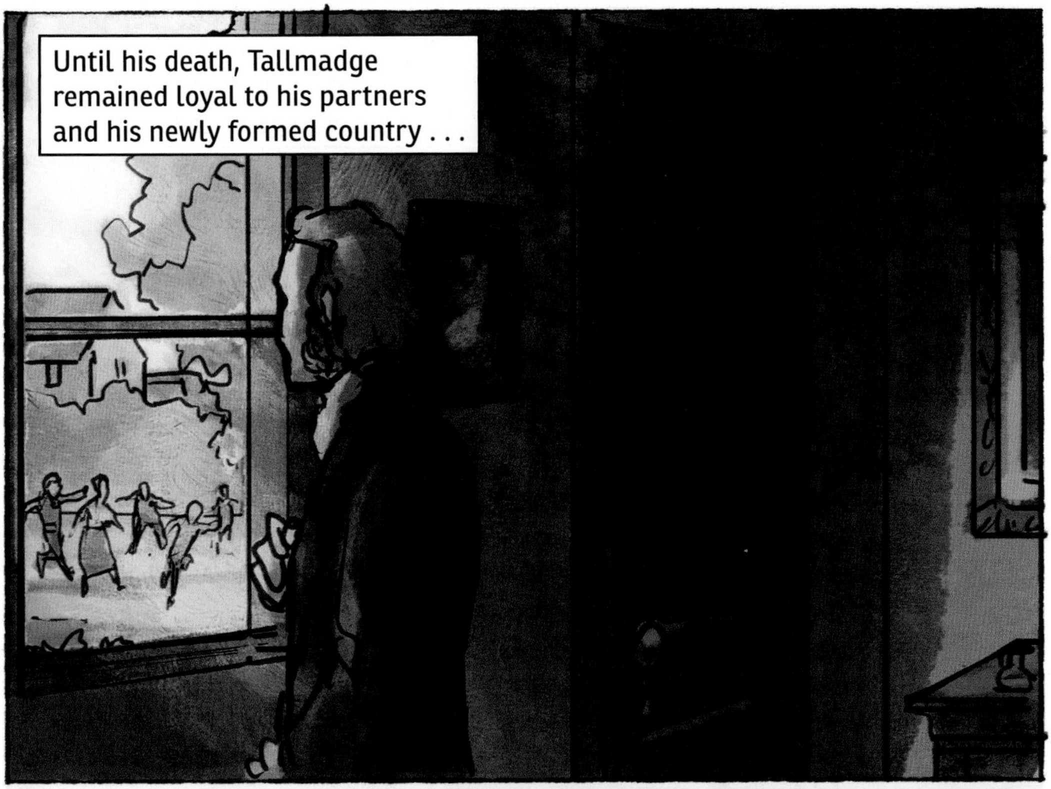
Until his death, Tallmadge remained loyal to his partners and his newly formed country . . .

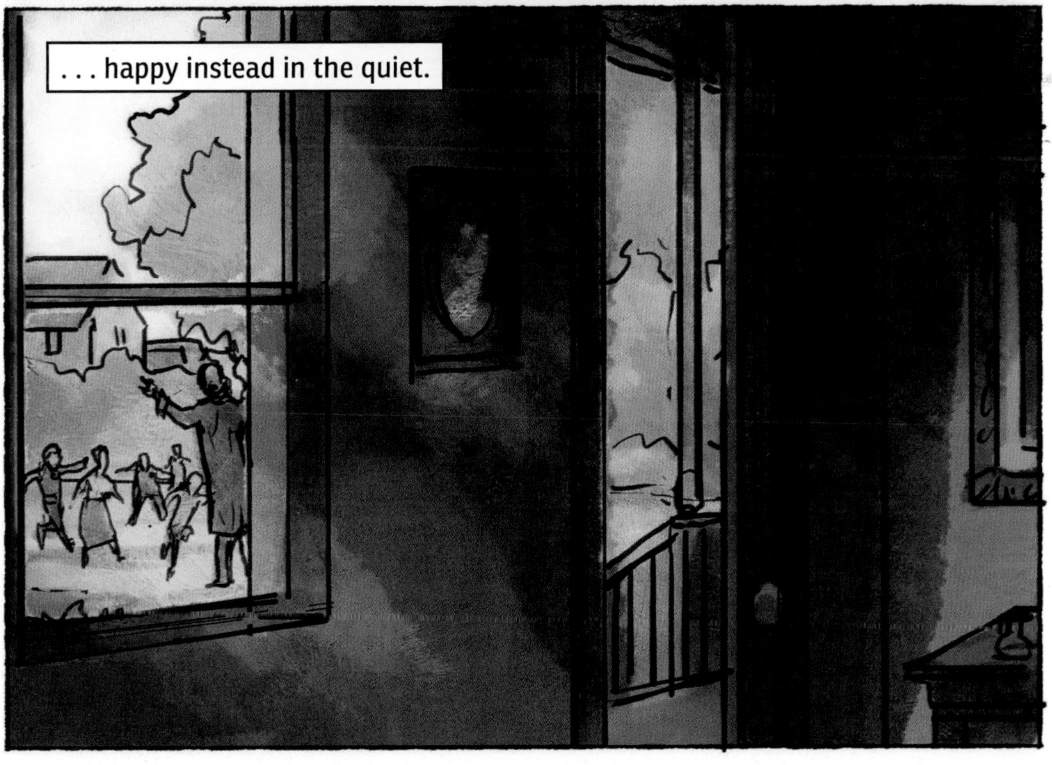
. . . happy instead in the quiet.

CHAPTER THREE

ANNA STRONG: THE SECRET SIGNAL

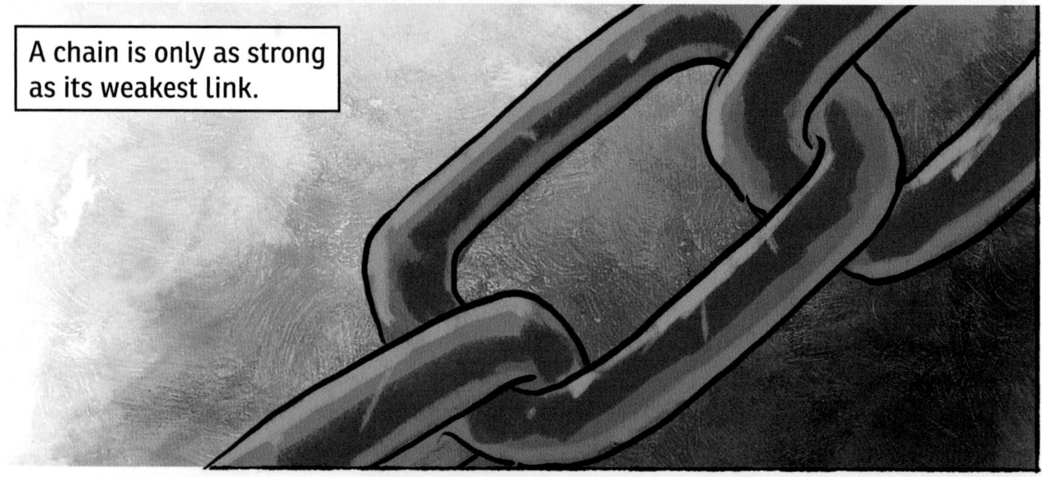
A chain is only as strong as its weakest link.

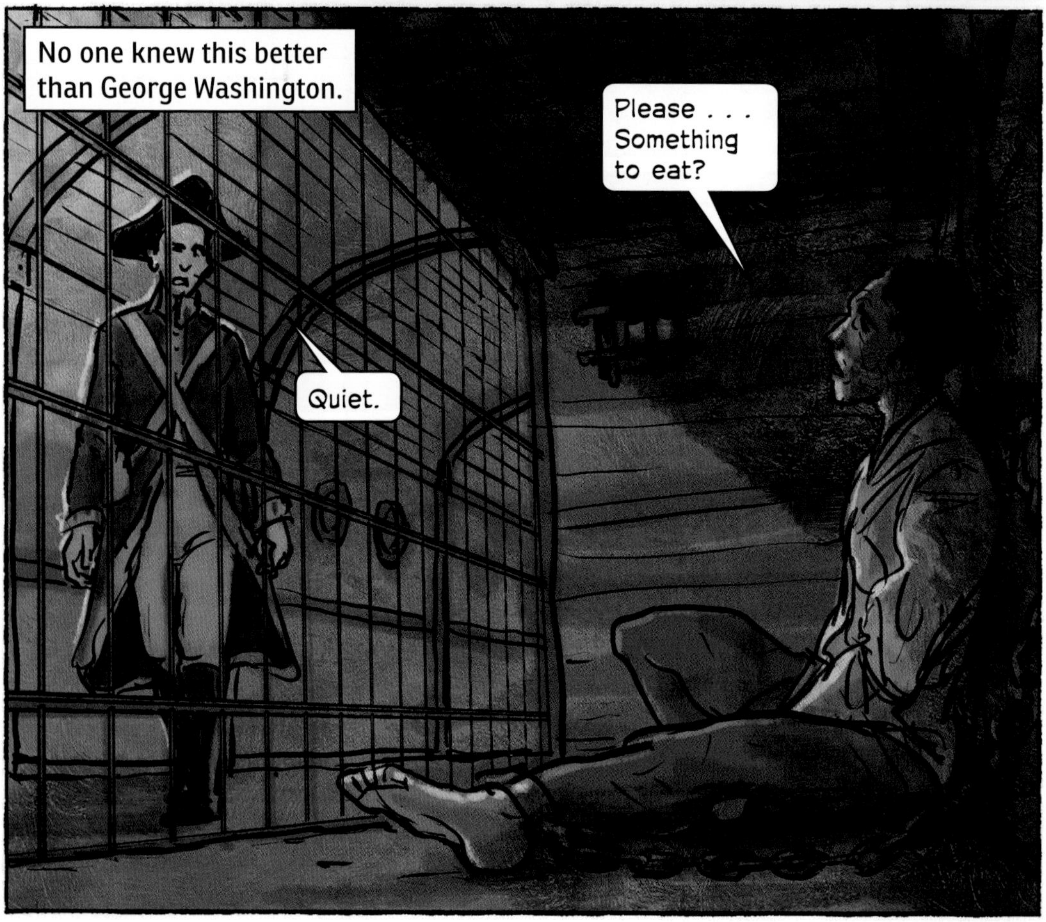
No one knew this better than George Washington.
Please . . . Something to eat?
Quiet.

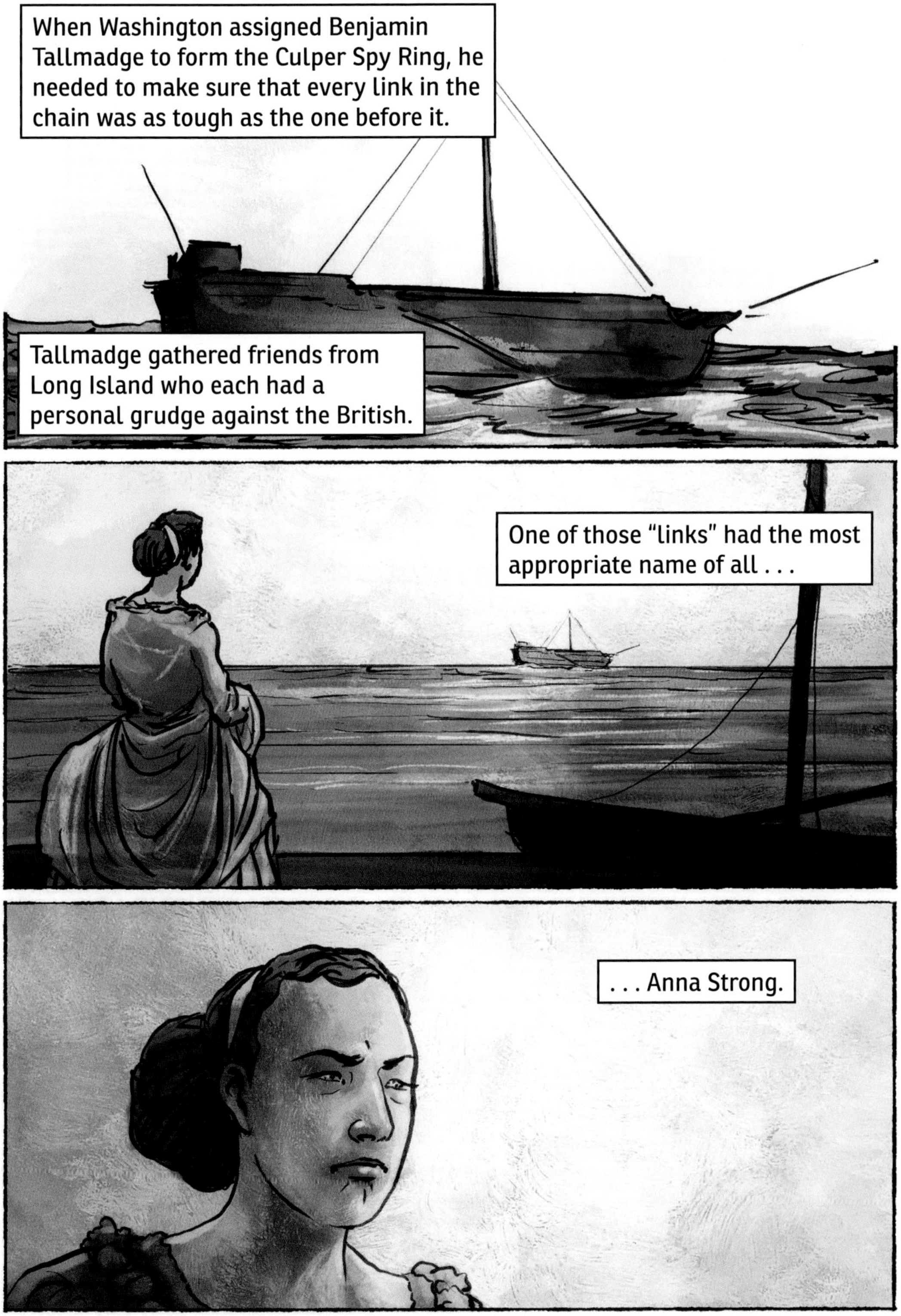
When Washington assigned Benjamin Tallmadge to form the Culper Spy Ring, he needed to make sure that every link in the chain was as tough as the one before it.
Tallmadge gathered friends from Long Island who each had a personal grudge against the British.
One of those "links" had the most appropriate name of all . . .
. . . Anna Strong.

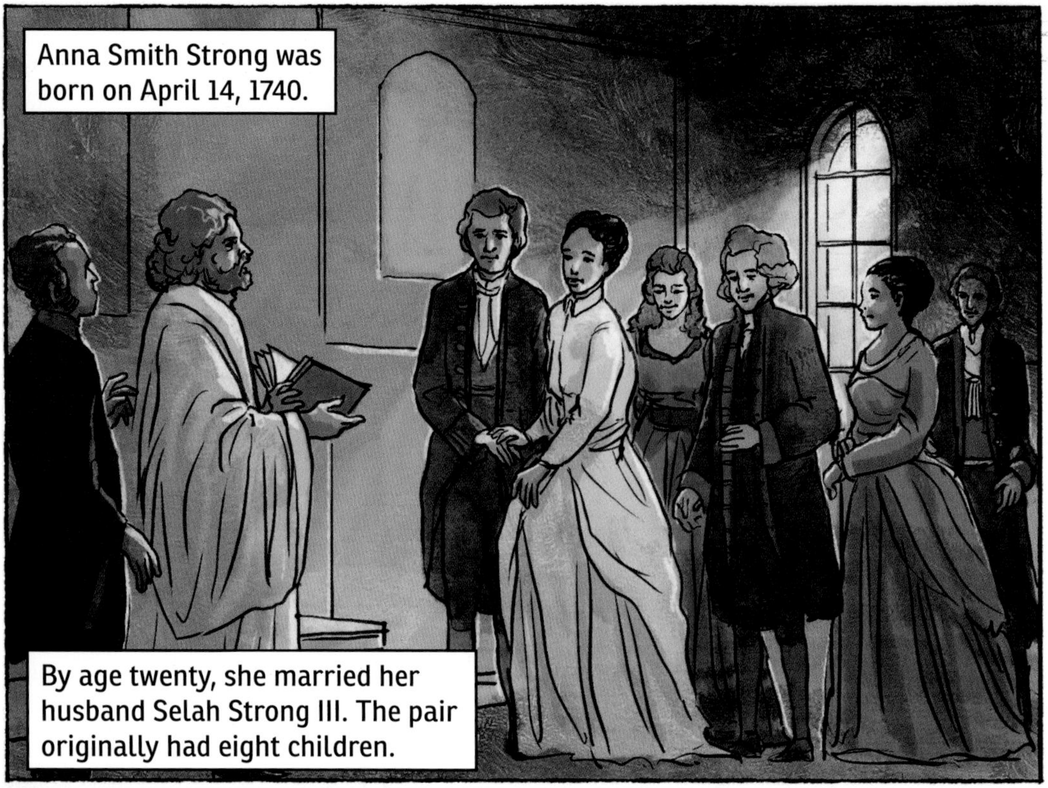
Anna Smith Strong was born on April 14, 1740.
By age twenty, she married her husband Selah Strong III. The pair originally had eight children.

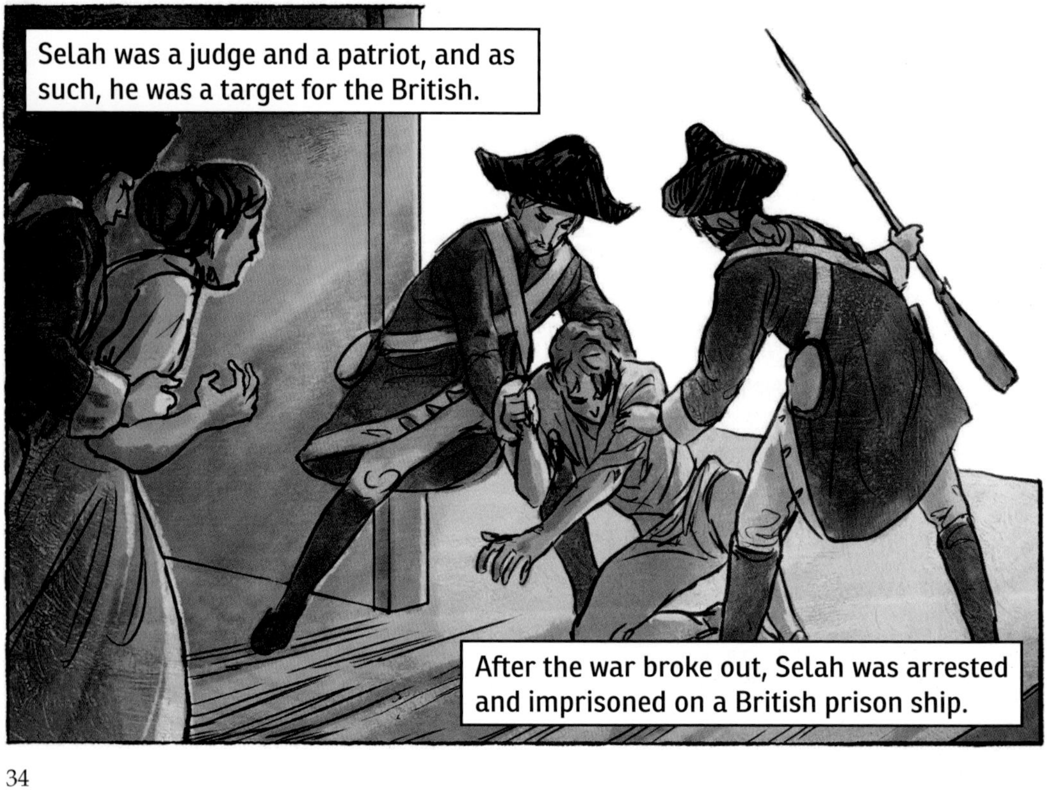
Selah was a judge and a patriot, and as such, he was a target for the British.
After the war broke out, Selah was arrested and imprisoned on a British prison ship.

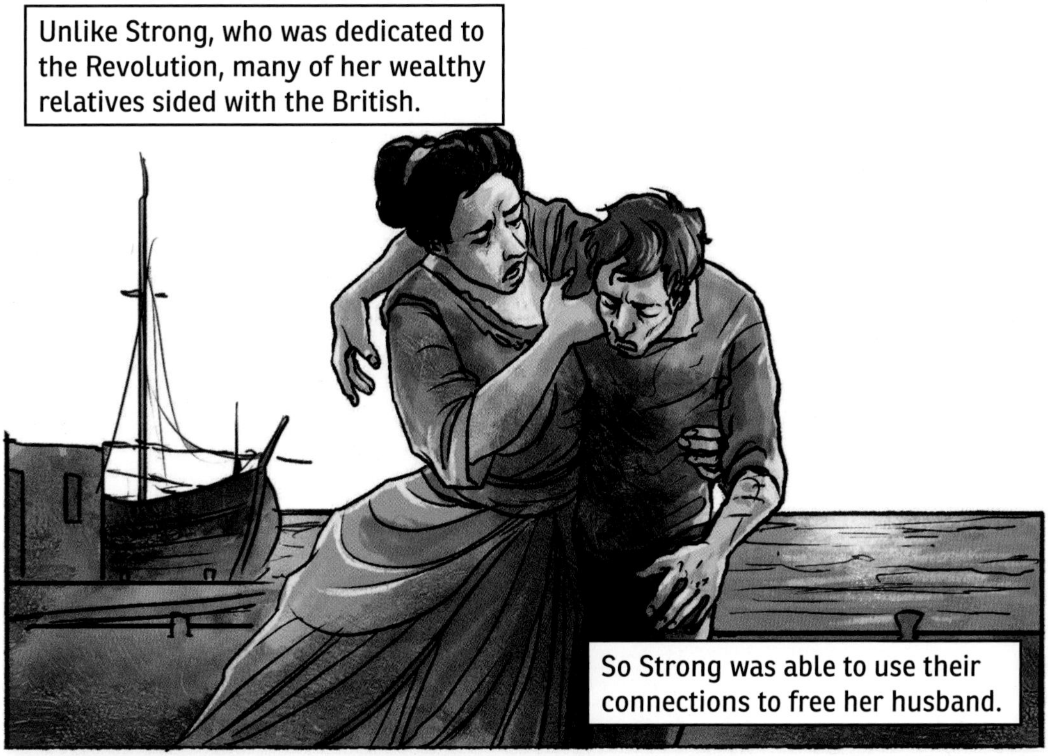
Unlike Strong, who was dedicated to the Revolution, many of her wealthy relatives sided with the British.
So Strong was able to use their connections to free her husband.

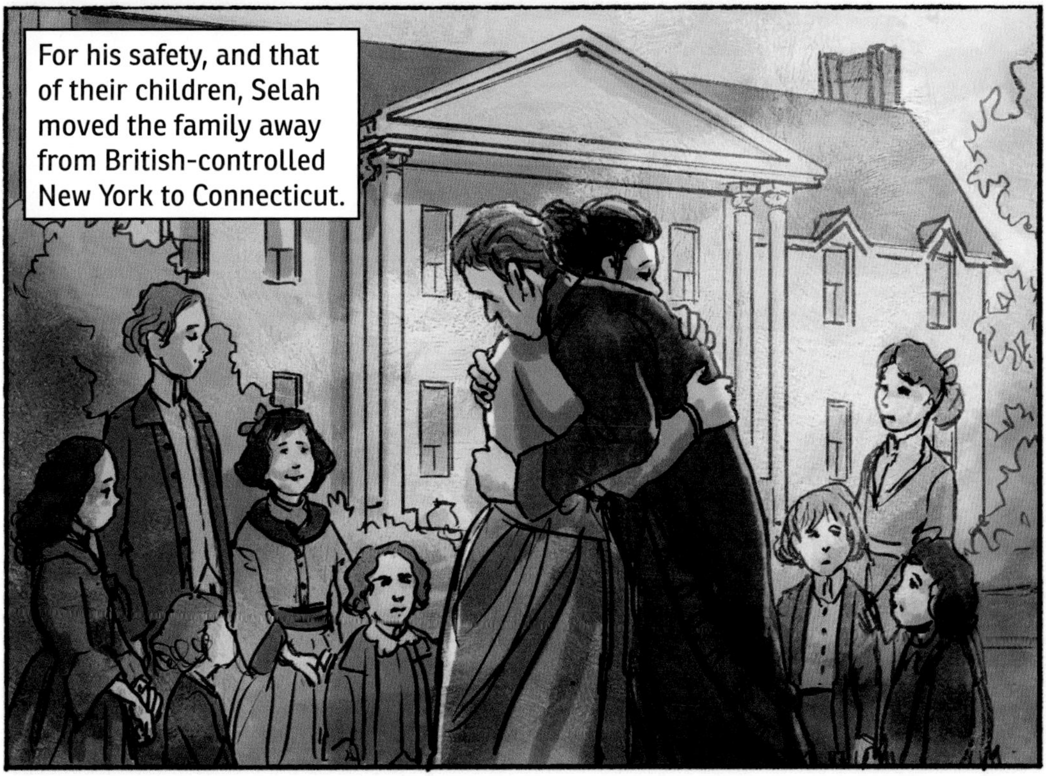
For his safety, and that of their children, Selah moved the family away from British-controlled New York to Connecticut.

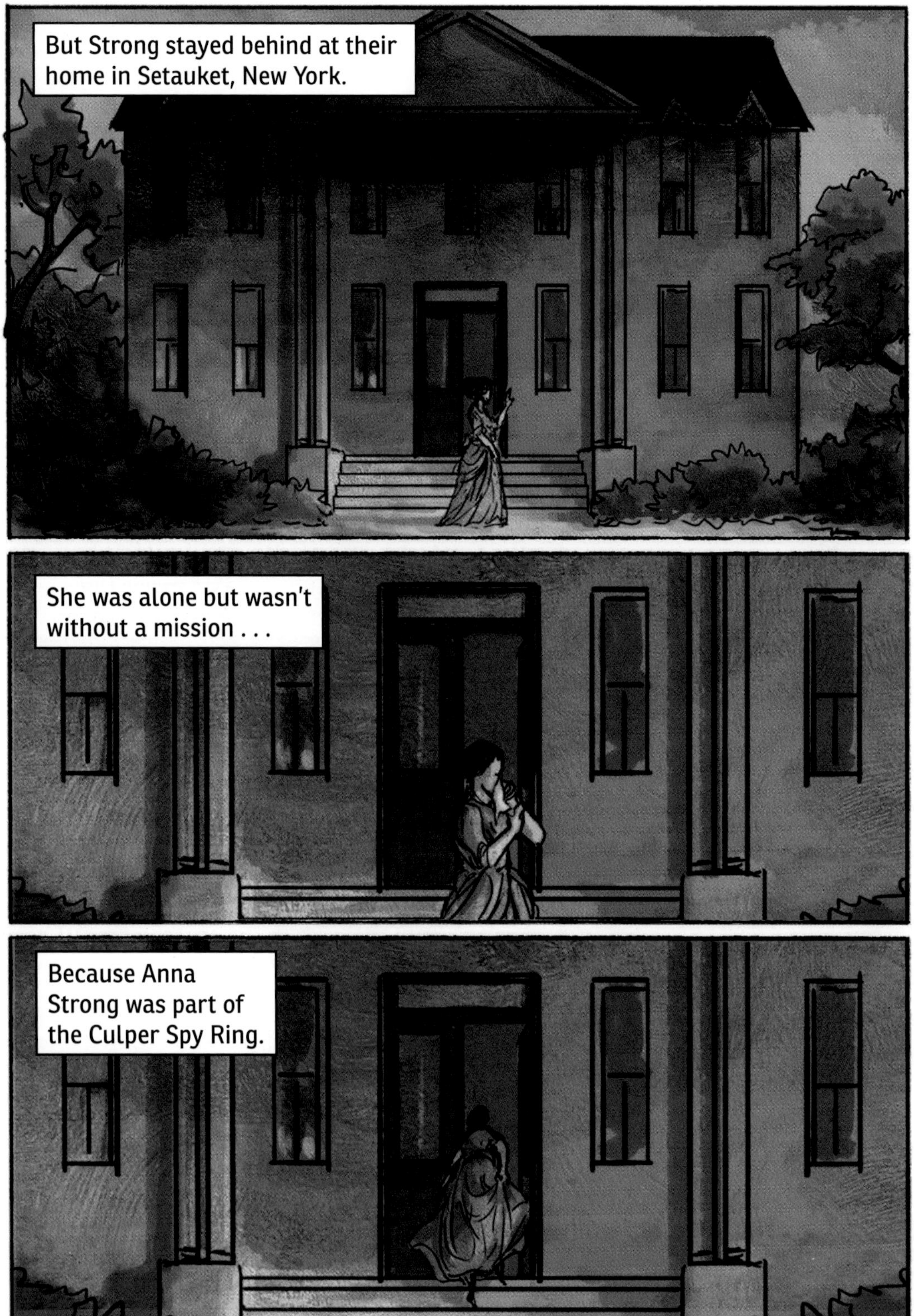
But Strong stayed behind at their home in Setauket, New York.
She was alone but wasn't without a mission . . .
Because Anna Strong was part of the Culper Spy Ring.

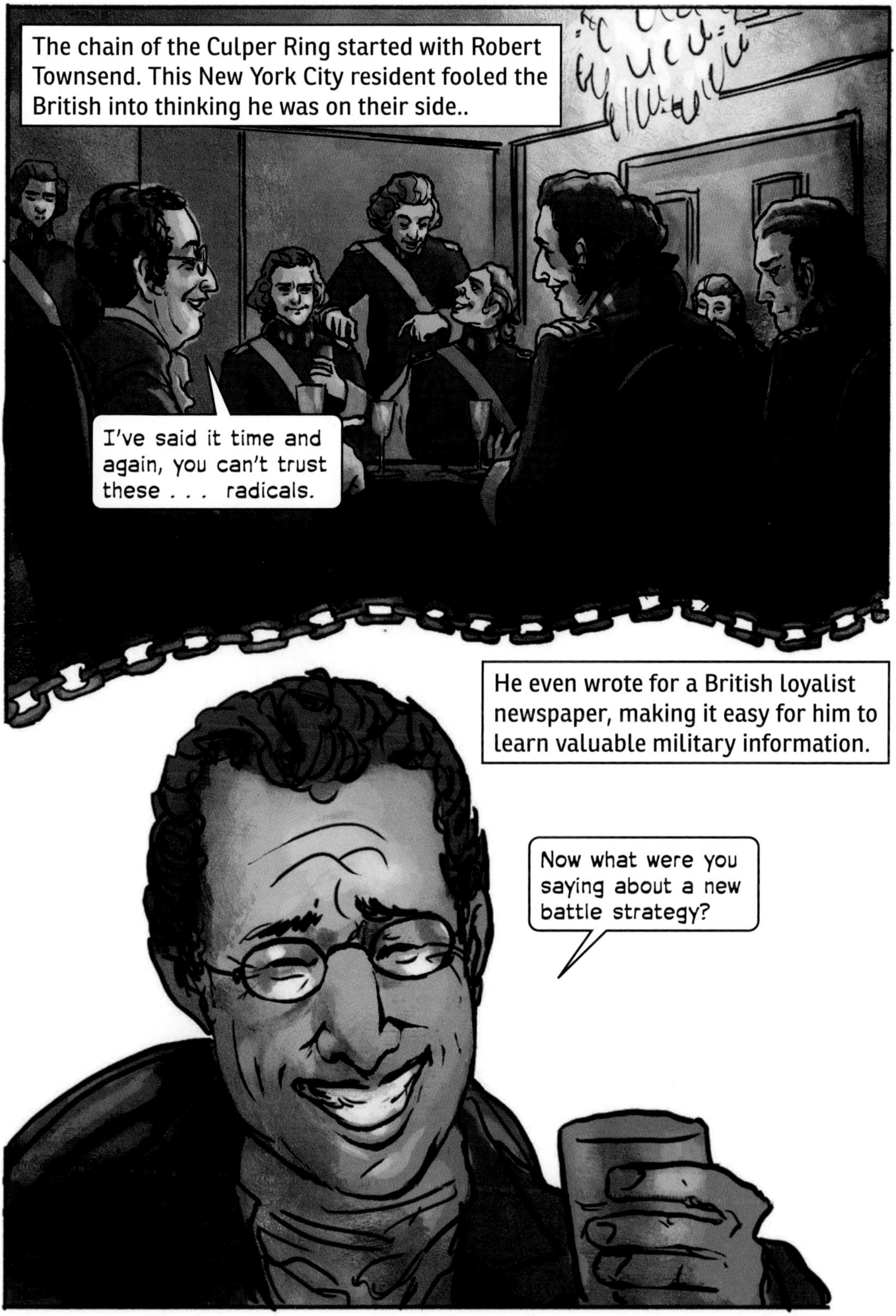
The chain of the Culper Ring started with Robert Townsend. This New York City resident fooled the British into thinking he was on their side..
I've said it time and again, you can't trust these . . . radicals.
He even wrote for a British loyalist newspaper, making it easy for him to learn valuable military information.
Now what were you saying about a new battle strategy?

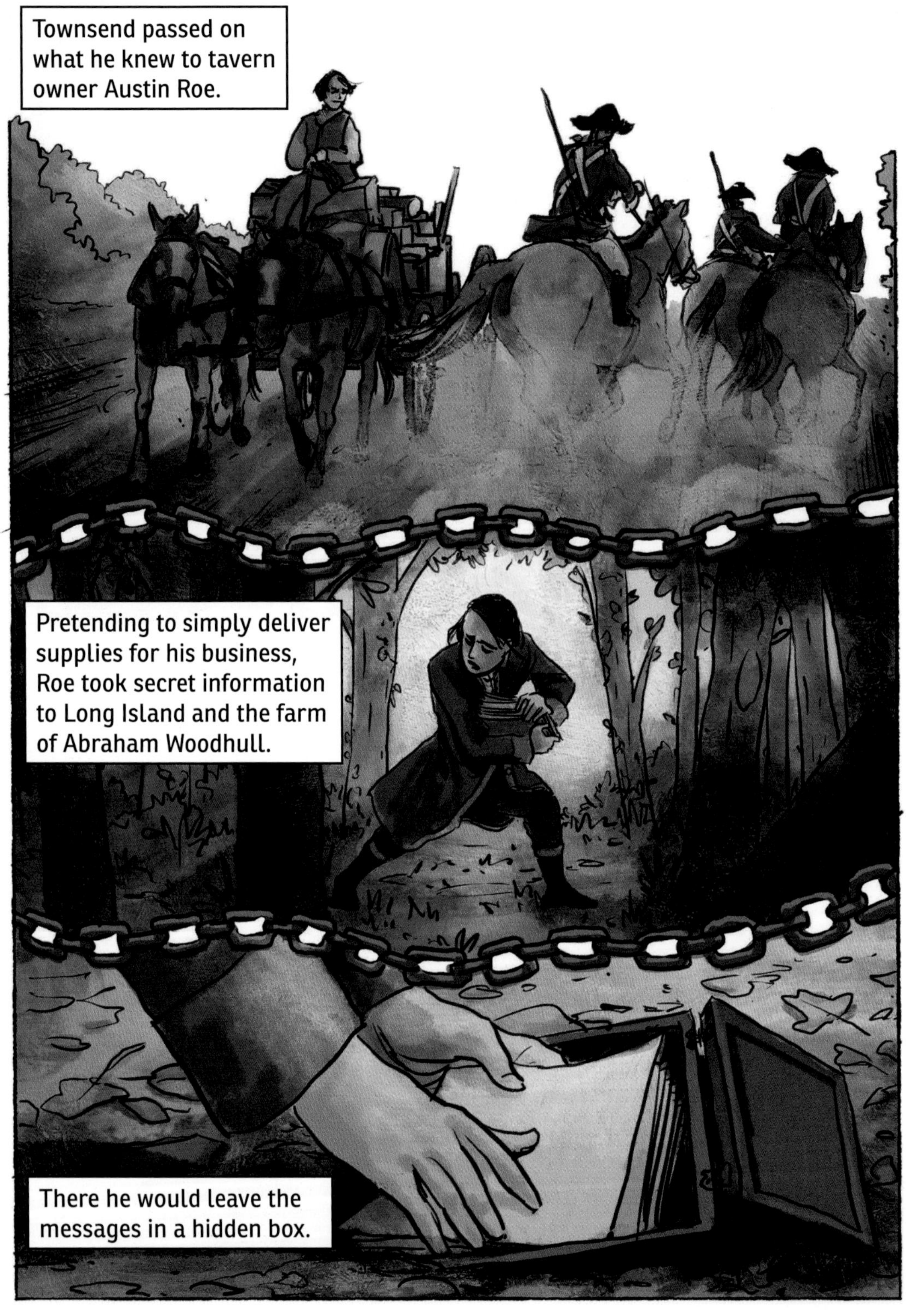
Townsend passed on what he knew to tavern owner Austin Roe.
Pretending to simply deliver supplies for his business, Roe took secret information to Long Island and the farm of Abraham Woodhull.
There he would leave the messages in a hidden box.

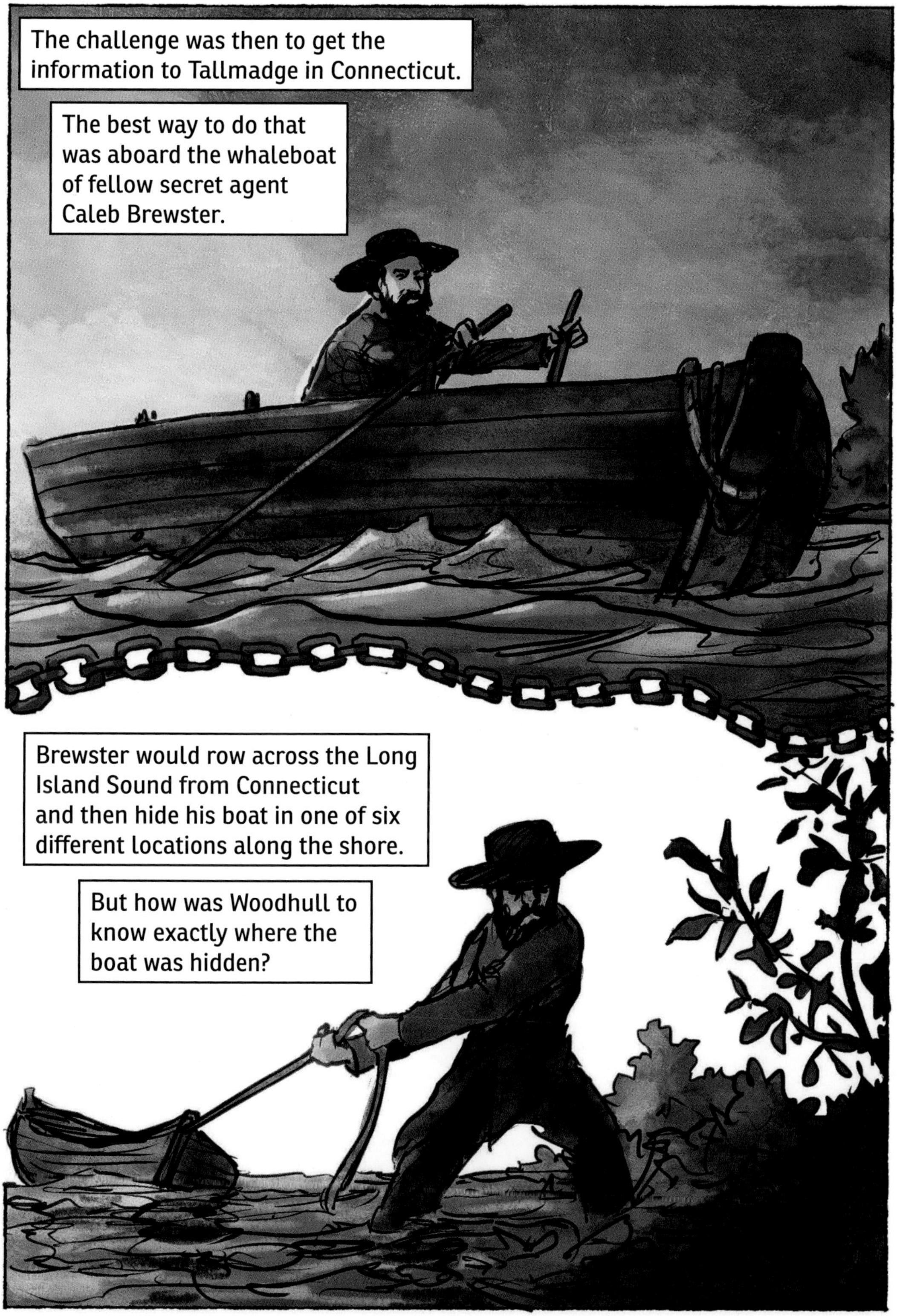
The challenge was then to get the information to Tallmadge in Connecticut.
The best way to do that was aboard the whaleboat of fellow secret agent Caleb Brewster.
Brewster would row across the Long Island Sound from Connecticut and then hide his boat in one of six different locations along the shore.
But how was Woodhull to know exactly where the boat was hidden?

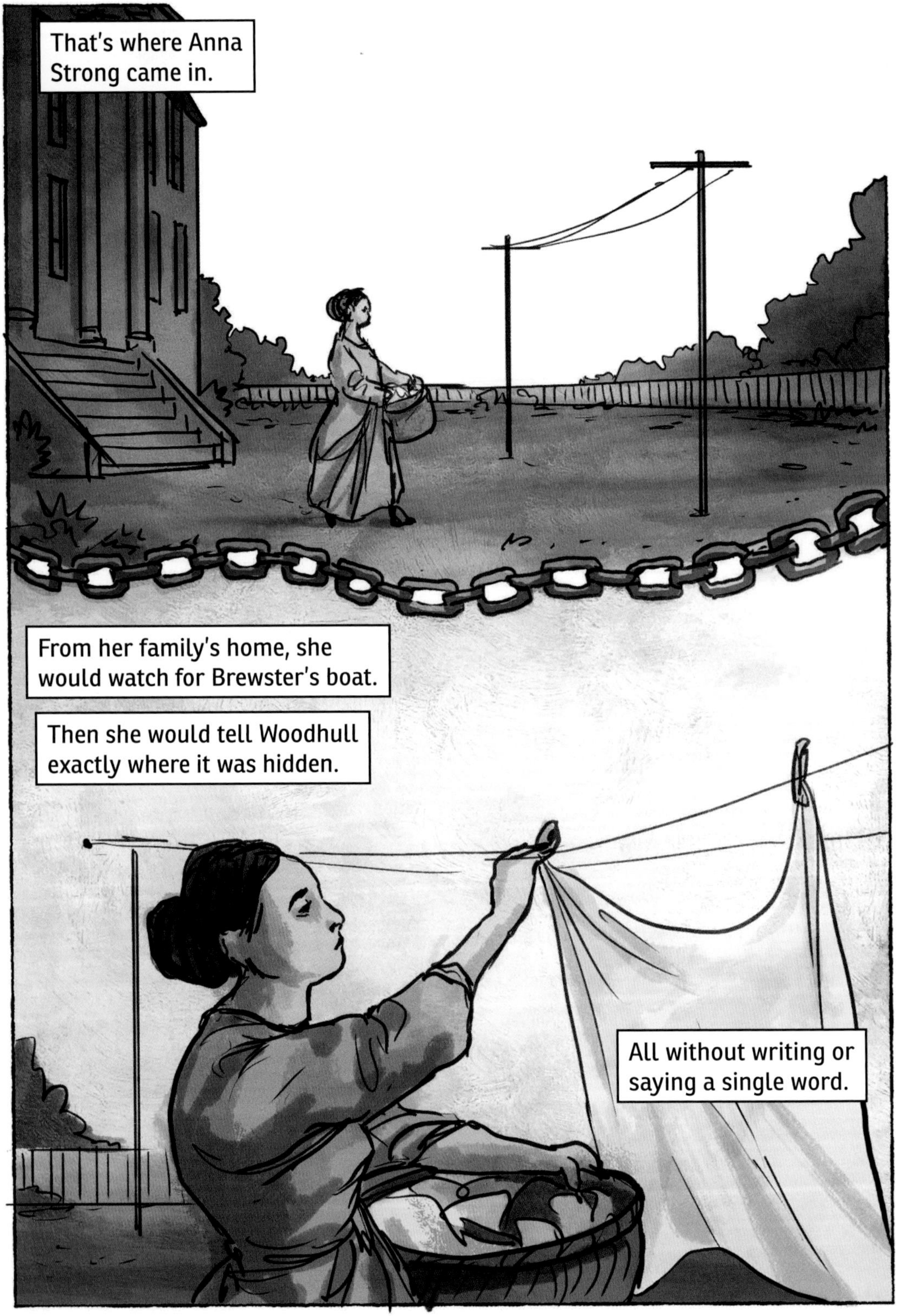
That's where Anna Strong came in.
From her family's home, she would watch for Brewster's boat.
Then she would tell Woodhull exactly where it was hidden.
All without writing or saying a single word.

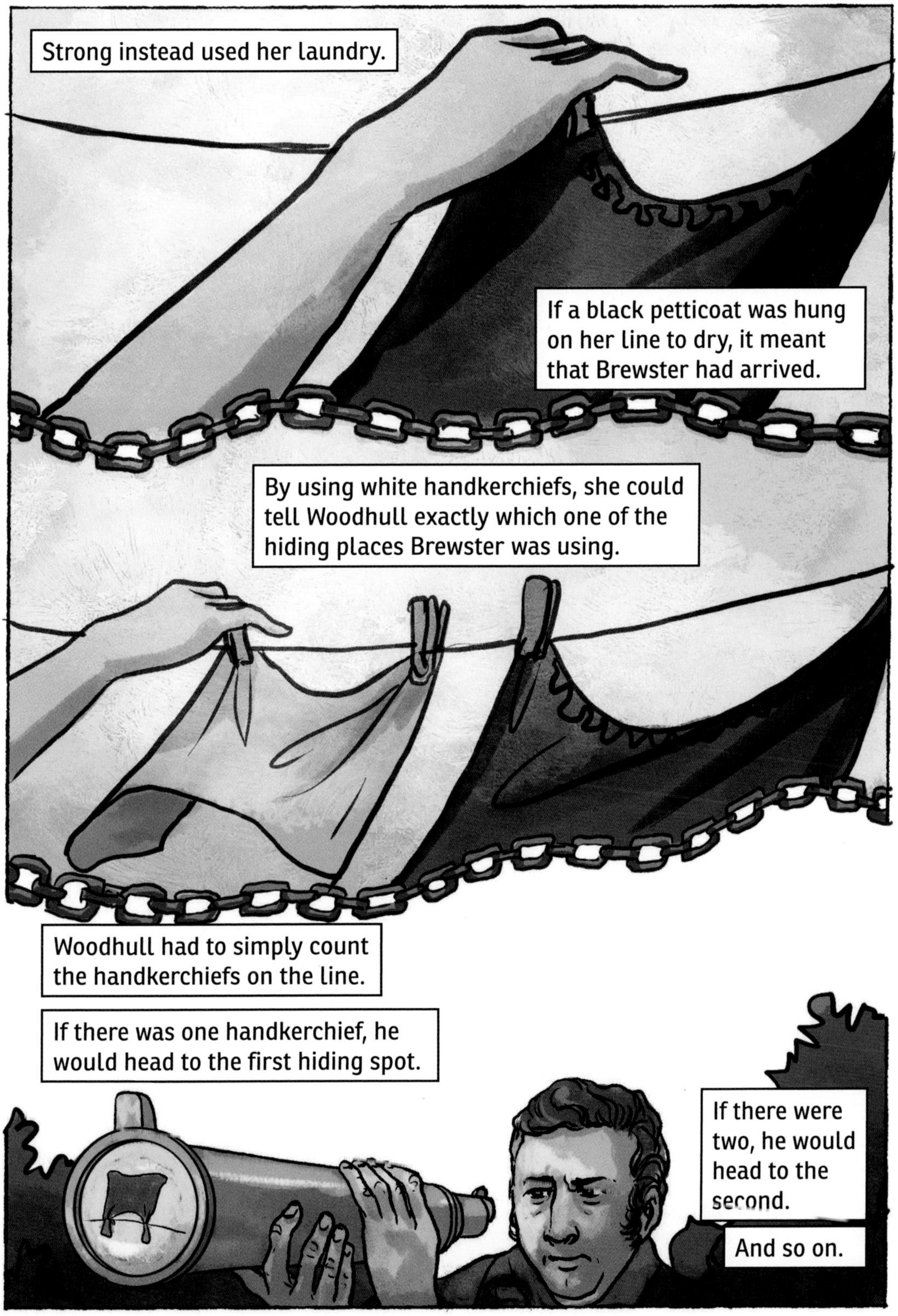
Strong instead used her laundry.
If a black petticoat was hung on her line to dry, it meant that Brewster had arrived.
By using white handkerchiefs, she could tell Woodhull exactly which one of the hiding places Brewster was using.
Woodhull had to simply count the handkerchiefs on the line.
If there was one handkerchief, he would head to the first hiding spot.
If there were two, he would head to the second.
And so on.

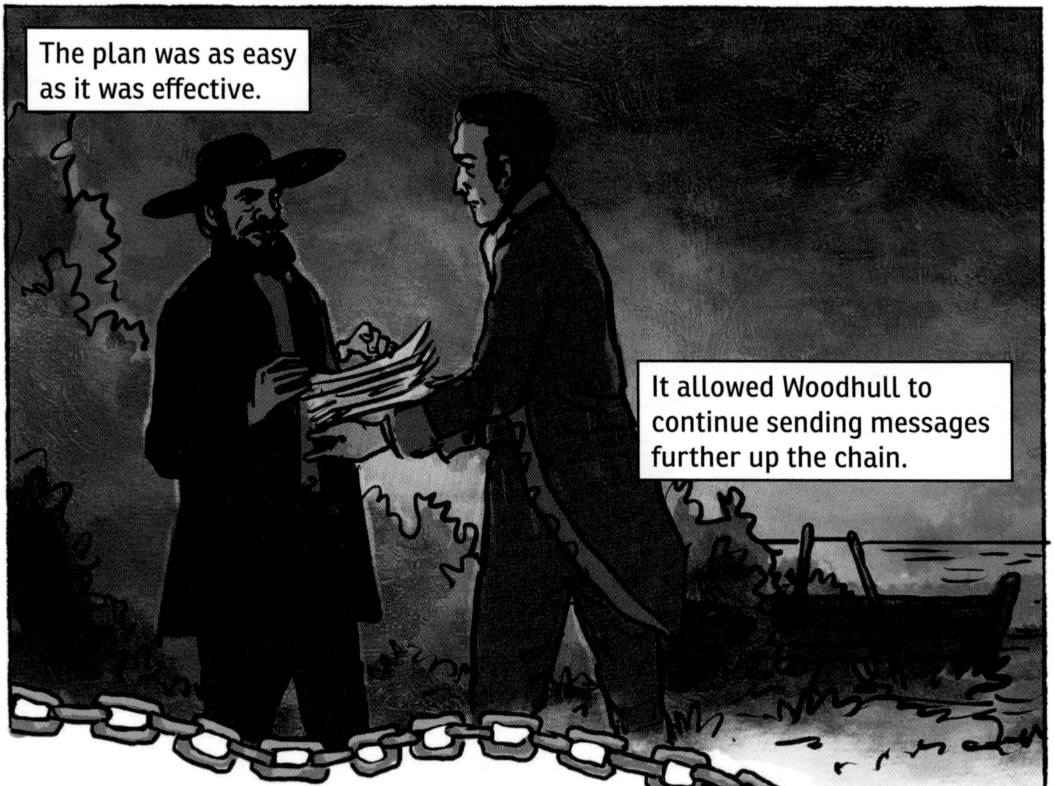
The plan was as easy as it was effective.
It allowed Woodhull to continue sending messages further up the chain.

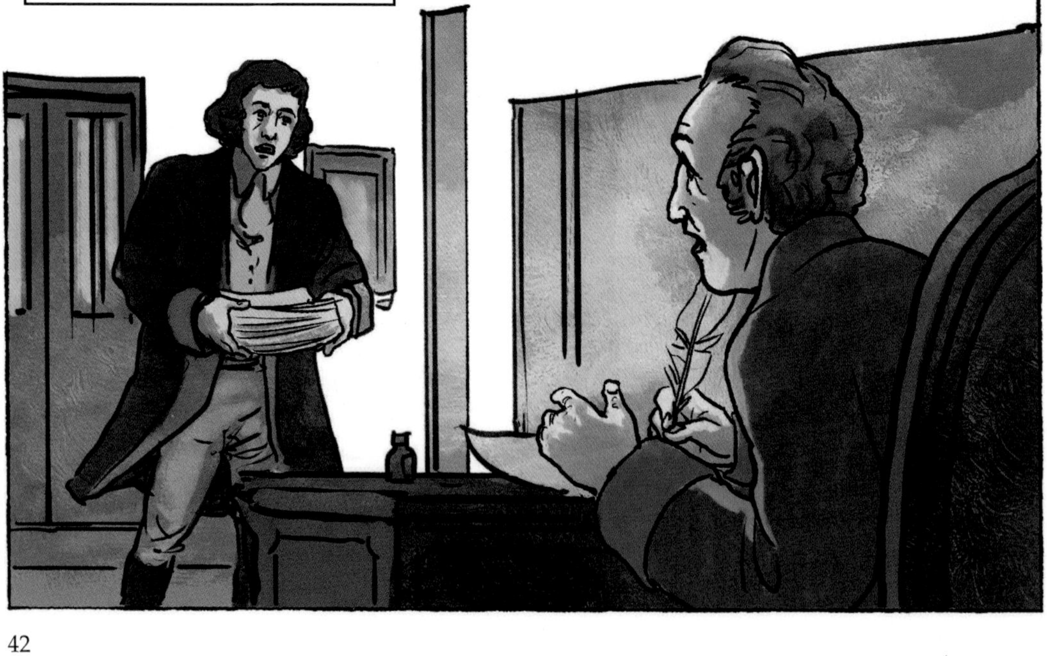
And soon enough, news from New York City would arrive safely in Connecticut.

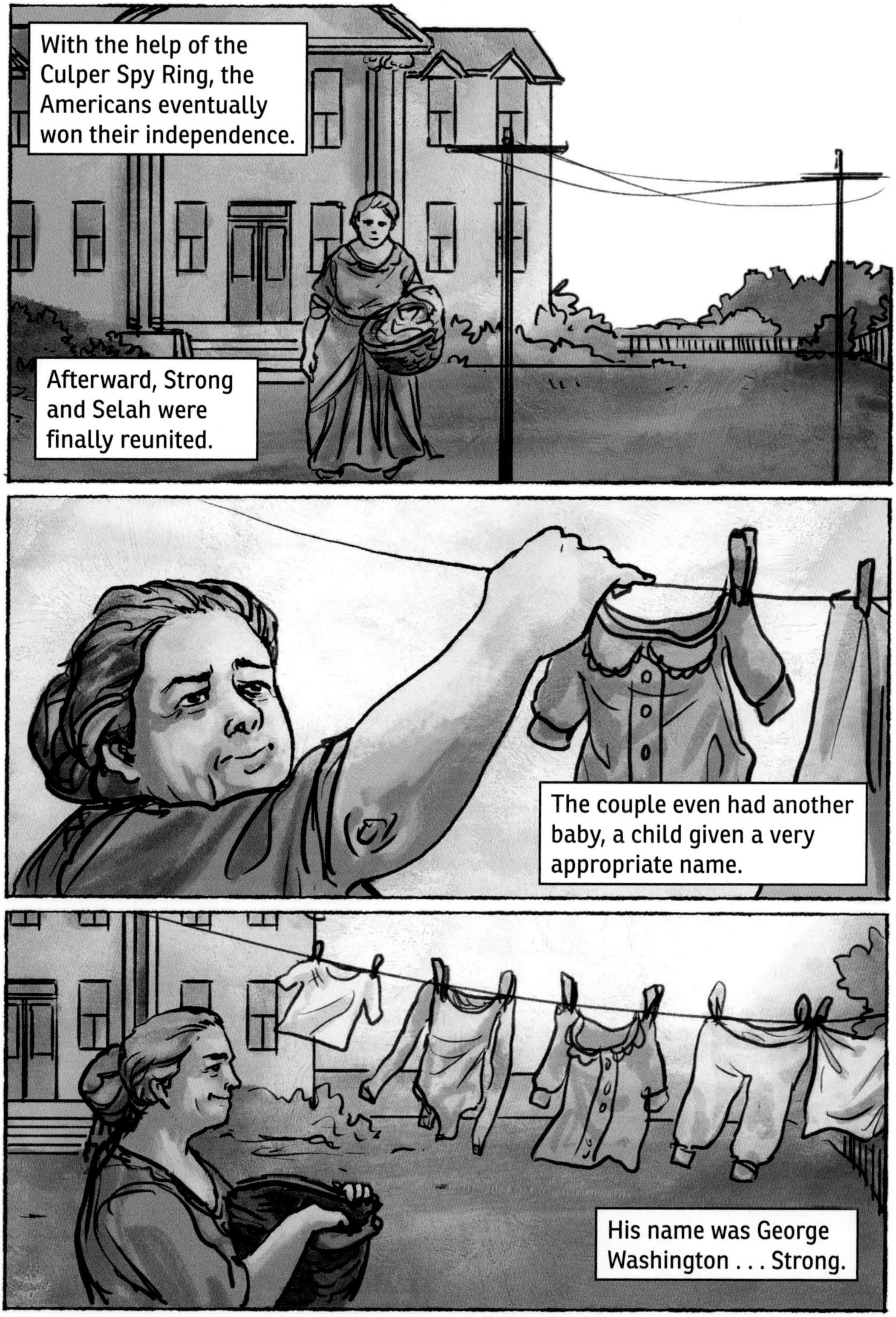
With the help of the Culper Spy Ring, the Americans eventually won their independence.
Afterward, Strong and Selah were finally reunited.
The couple even had another baby, a child given a very appropriate name.
His name was George Washington . . . Strong.

MORE ABOUT THE DARING SPIES OF THE AMERICAN REVOLUTION

- George Washington's Culper Spy Ring was named after Culpeper, a small community in Virginia where Washington had once worked.

- The Culper Ring wasn't Washington's only spy operation, but it received nearly a fourth of all the Continental funds dedicated to gathering intelligence.

- Benjamin Tallmadge was old friends with Nathan Hale, a spy who was famously hanged by the British. It is thought that Hale's death, along with the death of Benjamin's own brother, fueled Tallmadge's anger against the British.

- It wasn't unusual for Tallmadge to lead missions directly. His raid on British sympathizers encamped near Fort Franklin successfully rounded up nearly all the enemy without costing a single patriot's life.

- Anna Strong talked her way into bringing her husband food while he was imprisoned aboard a British prison ship. She later said that if she hadn't brought him something to eat, the British would've let him starve to death.

- In 1790, newly designated President George Washington went to Long Island, where he visited Anna Strong at the Roe Tavern. It wasn't stated at the time, but it is believed that Washington was there to secretly and personally thank the members of the invaluable Culper Spy Ring.

GLOSSARY

cipher (SY-fur)—a secret or disguised way of writing; a code

codes (KHODZ)—systems of words, letters, or symbols used to represent messages in a secret way

colonist (KOL-uh-nist)—a person who lives in a colony, which is a territory controlled by another country

dedicated (DED-i-kay-tid)—devoted to a task or purpose; having strong commitment

espionage (ES-pee-uh-nahzh)—the practice of spying or using spies to gather secret information

intelligence (in-TEL-i-juhns)—information gathered to understand and make decisions about enemy actions

legend (LEJ-uhnd)—a traditional story or myth, often about famous people or events

loyalist (LOY-uh-list)—a person who remains loyal to the established ruler or government, especially during a revolt

misinformation (mis-in-fer-MEY-shuhn)—false or inaccurate information spread intentionally or unintentionally

representation (rep-ri-zen-TEY-shuhn)—the act of speaking or acting on behalf of someone else

spymaster (SPAHY-mas-ter)—a person in charge of spies

strategy (STRAT-uh-jee)—a plan of action designed to achieve a long-term or overall goal

taxation (tak-SEY-shuhn)—the act of collecting money from citizens to pay for government services

READ MORE

Forest, Christopher. *The Rebellious Colonists and the Causes of the American Revolution.* North Mankato, MN: Capstone, 2022.

Gunderson, Jessica. *The Real Benedict Arnold: The Truth Behind the Legend.* North Mankato, MN: Capstone, 2020.

Kerry, Isaac. *The Battles of Lexington and Concord: A Day that Changed America.* North Mankato, MN: Capstone, 2023.

INTERNET SITES

Britannica Kids: American Revolution
kids.britannica.com/kids/article/American-Revolution/353711

Mount Vernon: American Spies of the Revolution
mountvernon.org/george-washington/the-revolutionary-war/spying-and-espionage/american-spies-of-the-revolution/

National Geographic Kids: Independence Day
kids.nationalgeographic.com/history/article/independence-day

ABOUT THE AUTHOR

PHOTO COURTESY OF
DOROTHY MANNING PHOTOGRAPHY

Matthew K. Manning is the author of more than 100 books and just as many comic books. Some of his favorite projects include the popular comic book crossover Batman/Teenage Mutant Ninja Turtles Adventures and the twelve-issue series Marvel Action: Avengers for IDW, *Exploring Gotham City* for Insight Editions, and the six-volume chapter book series Xander and the Rainbow-Barfing Unicorns for Capstone. Manning lives in Asheville, North Carolina, with his wife, Dorothy, and their two kids, Lilly and Gwen.

ABOUT THE ILLUSTRATOR

PHOTO COURTESY
OF DANTE GINEVRA

Dante Ginevra's work can be found in numerous publications in his home country of Argentina. These include comics and comic strips in *Fierro*, *Télam*, and a variety of other magazines. In addition, he has illustrative work in graphic novels that span the globe. They include *Cardal*, published in Uruguay, and *Entreactos* and *El Muertero Zabaletta*, both published in Spain. Throughout his career he has also participated in numerous exhibitions in Argentina, Italy, Russia, Brazil, France, and Germany.